Perspectives
on Mankind's
Search for Meaning

Walter Taminang

Sage Publishers, Inc.

5534 Stanton Ave, Suite 2

Pittsburgh, PA 15206

Perspectives on Mankind's Search for Meaning

First Printing, June 2008

Designed by Florence Tenguh Amandong MS, MBA

Published by Sage Publishers, Inc
Pittsburgh, PA 15206

ISBN: 978-0-6152-1981-3

Walter, Taminang.
  Perspectives on Mankind's Search for Meaning

Printed in the United States of America

Excerpts from First Light, copyright 1973 by Walter. H. Boore reprinted by kind permission of Continuum International Publishing Group.

The Author

Walter Taminang, MD is a research fellow at the department of Pulmonary and Critical Care Medicine at the University of Pittsburgh Medical Center, Pennsylvania state, USA. He represents a rare breed of contemporary scientists with diverse intellectual interests that extend far beyond the confines of science. In this book, Taminang draws upon his immense grasp of science, religion, theology, philosophy, anthropology and his own personal experiences to bring forth a new and refreshing perspective of religion and spirituality. In writing this book, he portrays a deep understanding of life's big questions and contradictions. In his spare time he enjoys reading, writing and traveling.

To

-my father, who taught me to be courageous and to love learning;
-my mother, for her constant love, devotion, and purity of soul;
-my brother Fidelis Muki Taminang, who believed in me, loved life but left it too soon.

Acknowledgements

This work began in 2006 in the form of serial postings titled "The Search for Truth", broadcast on *Eden newspaper*, and CRTV Buea in 2006. The resultant media exposure and stimulating feedback from fans and pundits were among the factors that encouraged me to develop and publish this work.

My heartfelt appreciation goes to Mr John Fombang of United Nations, Tanzania, for his sustained public and private endorsements of my literary endeavors. His gentle reminders during the writing process jolted me out of occasional writer's fatigue to stay the course and complete this project.

My sincere gratitude goes to Florence Tenguh Amandong of Pittsburgh, Pennsylvania State, U.S.A for proof-reading, formatting, and designing the manuscript.

So many people, too numerous to mention here, but who know themselves offered so much encouragement by their words, comments and letters, and I owe so much to so many for their contributions in this regard.

As always, I am very grateful to my family, to our Ancestors and to the God of the universe for their presence and work through my life.

To Sage Publishers Inc., readers and this wonderful country, thank you for believing in me.

CONTENTS

Walter Taminang

There is only one highest reality and many teachers
All human life arises from the same source
All countries, religions and institutions arise from that
There are many books of wisdom from many ages
Thinking there is only one way comes from ignorance
Coercive conversion is violence against other peoples
The goal of life is found within, not in institutions
Wisdom, joy, and freedom come from inner stillness
Love all, as we are all waves of the one ocean.

Prologue

We are entering a period when very small numbers of persons, operating with enormous power of modern computers, biogenetics, air transport, and even small nuclear weapons, can deal lethal blows to any society.

-Philip Bobbit, 2002

The history of the human race is a sad tale of conflict, brutality, violence, and wars, interspersed with periods of peace, creativity and technical growth. The world religions were in retreat 40 years ago with the remorseless march of western secularism and atheistic communism dominant in Asia. Almost all denominations have witnessed a remarkable revival over the past quarter century. A new wave of religiously-based conflicts has come with religious revivalism. Currently, there are at least 18 hotspots of religious-based conflict in the world - some new, some very old; [1] the war in Iraq, now in its fifth year, is being heightened by religious and ethnic conflict. A number of spectacular attacks by Islamic militants on the World Trade Center and the Pentagon in 2001, on a Bali nightclub in 2002, and on Madrid railway targets in 2004, have been accompanied by regular killings, bomb attacks and other atrocities. The militant groups, particularly Al-Qaeda, led by Osama bin Laden, have declared holy war against the West and are committed to reducing Western influence in the Islamic world. Hundreds of young Muslims have died in suicide attacks.

This religious revival has also affected Christianity. In the USA, eligious fundamentalism has also become an important political force both in foreign policy and internal politics, where popular Christianity has challenged the accepted orthodoxies of secular, rationalist science. Just like Christianity split into Catholics and Protestants in the 16th century, Islam now has to contend with a sharpening split between Sunni and Shia. In Afghanistan and Pakistan, extreme radical fundamentalist Muslim terrorist groups clash perpetually with non-Muslims and moderates. The protracted middle-east crisis between Muslims, Jews, and Christians seem to have no end in sight. In Kashmir the clash between Hindus and Muslims has claimed thirty to sixty thousand people since 1989. In India, various conflicts heat up periodically between Animists, Hindus, Muslims and Sikhs producing loss of life. In Northern Ireland, tensions are partly rooted in Catholic/Protestant differences, partly in political allegiances, and partly in hatreds that stretch so far back that the exact reason is lost in the mists of time. In the former Yugoslavia an uneasy peace reigns, but tensions between Catholics, Muslims, and Orthodox Christians played a part in the civil war of the 1990s, and remain an issue that divides not only the Balkans, but the Caucasus and southern Russia. The war in Bosnia-Herzegovina was among three faith groups (Muslim, Roman Catholic, and Serbian Orthodox). The civil war in Sudan has a significant religious component. Ignited in 1983, the civil war there has killed some 2 million people and displaced more than four million. In Nigeria, Yoruba and Christians in the south of the country are battling Muslims in the north. The country is struggling towards democracy after decades of Muslim military dictatorships. Religious conflicts have become the major force for destabilizing world politics, and will remain so among the youthful and disillusioned populations of the world if something urgent is not done.

Conflicts have always been an integral part of the human condition. Intra-organizational and intra-faith conflicts result from different viewpoints regarding life's meaning, our place in the world, our relationship with each other and with our creator. Conflicts are not necessarily bad. Effective resolution of conflicts can actually lend new paradigms and fresher perspectives on troubling issues. It is our ability or inability to manage conflicts that determine the consequences, good or evil. In order to effectively resolve conflicts, we have to be ready to dig to the root of issues to find out why things happen or what we must do to change them. This of course takes time and effort. Most people in the world are taught - either by their parents, their school, and their country or by custom or religion, to hang on to their *differences* with others. Examples abound. Men and women easily see differences between themselves, but with more difficulty find their similarities. Racial problems and turbulence are based on one or both races placing too much emphasis on their differences. Ethnic differences can bring the same result. Different political approaches to governing where one kind of government attempts to impose its approach of governing on other states can bring a similar result. This is the case with religions as well. Each religion is based on the concept that it has the answer to the mystery of life and death; and since there is only one solution to any mystery, this implies that when "my religion has the answer, all other answers are wrong". This creates resentment which festers with time, leading to conflicts, followed by violence with its ensuing tragic results. We see it every day. But we are no closer to solving the problem now than we were hundreds of years ago. Why is this so?

In the course of human development mankind has increasingly relied on science and religion to answer life's most serious questions. Science applies reason while religion applies faith. Reason alone cannot answer all the questions that human beings are capable of asking. Science is not particularly suited to dealing with problems of human existence that have no enduring logical or factual solution, such as avoiding death, overcoming loneliness, finding love, or ensuring justice. Science cannot tell us what we *ought* to do or what we should be. It can only inform us about what is and what we *can* do. Science looks at natural phenomena and attempts to explain *how* they occur, while religion deals with the supernatural realm and attempts to explain *why*. No amount of thinking can resolve serious questions such as "what is the meaning of life?" or "what is consciousness?" or "is there life after death?" Those who cannot live with the unavoidable doubts that come with a life of pure reason often resort to religious faith, either seeking comfort from God in the face of the unknown (and unknowable), or in the hopes of finding answers to these mysteries in the scripture. Faith is a very strong passion, for better or worse. On the one hand, faith in divine justice or simply happy endings help some people endure the unendurable without making matters worse for others. Yet faith can also impel people to seek a violent death for themselves and others, leaving the world a worse place than they found it. So if someone says he has great faith, that person holds a two-edged sword. Faith often prevents the exercise of reason, making it a strong yet also potentially blinding passion.

By contrast, doubt is an important tool in exercising reason, and is complementary to faith. Therefore people who rely exclusively on faith limit their capacity to make deep philosophical inquiries, leaving them, perhaps passionately wedded to superstitions and fairy tales. Having faith does not totally eliminate doubt. But it may cause the staunch believer to conceal doubt which ultimately leads to unhappiness. But uncertainty and unhappiness, or commitment to superstitions, especially if shared by large groups, can lead to bigotry, even fanatical intolerance, and definitely unreasonable behavior. People of faith suppressing their own doubts often seek to impose their views on everyone, in the vain hope that this will lessen their doubts. It never does of course. In my opinion, the acid test of anyone's faith is whether they can simply worship in peace, without attempting to embroil or coerce the world in their enterprise.

Religion thrives because it addresses our deepest emotional yearnings and the society's foundational moral needs. No society has ever lasted more than a few generations without a moral foundation that, though rationally inscrutable, is considered to be unquestionably true. Science, therefore, may never completely replace religion in the lives of most people, or in any society that hopes to survive for very long; neither can religion replace science if humankind hopes to unlock nature's material secrets. Religious fervor is, if anything, increasing across the world. The proportion of people attached to the world's four biggest religions - Christianity, Islam, Buddhism and Hinduism-rose from 67% in 1900 to73% in 2005 and may reach 80% by 2050[2]. According to the most recent surveys, 95 percent of Americans believe in God, more than two-thirds belong to a church. 60% of Americans say God plays an important role in their lives, and 37% call themselves committed Christians [3]. Philip Jenkins, one of America's best scholars of religion, claims that when historians look back at this century, they will probably see religion as "the prime animating and destructive force in human affairs, guiding attitudes to political liberty and obligation, concepts of nationhood, and, of course, conflicts and wars". If things should continue at the same pace with the first seven years of the century, Mr. Jenkins may well turn out to be right. An underlying reason is that science treats humans and their intentions only as incidental elements in the universe, whereas in religion, humans are central. Personal gods speak to personal problems - perhaps even more so in complex and mobile societies increasingly divorced from nurturing family settings and long-familiar environments.

It is my belief that successful living is nothing more or less than the art of the mastery of dependable techniques for solving common problems. The first step in the solution of any problem is to locate the difficulty, to isolate the problem, and frankly to recognize its nature and gravity. The great mistake is that, when life problems excite our profound fears, we refuse to recognize them. Likewise, when the acknowledgment of our difficulties entails the reduction of our long-cherished conceit, or the abandonment of deep-seated prejudices, the average person prefers to cling to the old illusions of safety and to the long-cherished false feelings of security. Only a brave person is honestly willing to admit and fearlessly face what a sincere and logical mind discovers.

With the rising tide of global religious fundamentalism, it is important that we realize the real dangers we face as citizens of the world. If this ugly trend should continue, our specie faces a real threat of complete and mutually-assured annihilation. It is becoming increasingly evident that the human race is under immense pressure to evolve to a new way of thinking; a higher level of consciousness. By fervent questioning and seeking with the hope of finding, I believe we can all know the truth. I believe the best way of beginning the quest is to carefully examine the very foundations of our current belief systems.

Walter Taminang

This book is not an endorsement of blind belief, but a denial of disbelief. In the modern world such perhaps, is the best definition of faith. While mutually exclusive positives compete in separated disciplines, assertive advertisements, dogmatic sects, sovereign states, party politics, public works and private enterprise, perhaps certainty can rest only in the double negative. In writing this book, I hope to awaken us to the reality of our basic spirituality which lies at the inner core of our beings irrespective of our religious sect or denomination. Such spiritual enlightenment I believe could be a first essential step towards increased religious tolerance and sustainable world peace.

1

The Search for Truth

Two sorts of truths: Profound truths recognized by the fact that the opposite is also a profound truth, in contrast to trivialities where opposites are obviously absurd.

Niels Bohr (1885-1962). Danish nuclear physicist

Science deals mainly with facts; religion deals mainly with values. The two are not rivals. They are complementary.

Martin Luther King, Jr (1929-1968). Strength to Love, 1.1, 1963

Mankind has sought for truth in three main ways -through science, through art, and through religion; by doubt, by vision, and by faith. Science analyses; art embraces; religion sublimates: Science walks backwards from what it has discovered; art forwards to what it seeks; religion accompanies what it believes. The values of science are quantitative - it measures; of art, qualitative - it appreciates; of religion, transcendent - it enhances. Science seeks uniformity of function whereas art discovers uniqueness of performance. Laboratory repetition corroborates; whereas in religion, art or psychic research, repetition impugns. There are dozens of ways of comparing and contrasting the three, each correct in its own context; but the truth of each exceeds definition; and the triple truth is greater than the three together.

It may be that science, to which all data are equivalent, lacks value and significance; that art, in which all factors are eclectic, lacks assessment and consummation; and that religion, in which all things are glorified, lacks proportion and development: but they make up for each other. And there is something more than these three provinces of man; and that is man himself. As the scientist proves his hypotheses by experiment, so the devotee justifies his assumptions by experience. And none can deny that both find ample confirmation. But both may not be wholly undeceived; could it not be that experience may contain working out of belief in the same way as experiment may contain the imposition of pattern? However, if the experience of religion in life confirms for some of its truth, so does the exercise of religion in church bring assurance to the worshipper. How far the worshipper is drugged by ritual, consoled by familiarity, bemused by homily, strengthened by song or warmed by prayer into a state of hypnotic awareness is hard to say; or whether he is spiritually recharged by going once a week to the edge of the world to look over. Deprecate if we like the blind confusion of sacrament with reality, we cannot ignore the poetry of worship. And of course, the God of love who taught kindness as the way to it may recognize in 'services' the first steps to the love of God.

Early science such as geometry and astronomy was connected to the divine for most medieval scholars. The compass in this 13th century manuscript is a symbol of God's act of creation.The scientific method gains knowledge by testing hypotheses to develop theories through elucidation of facts or evaluation by experiments and thus only answers cosmological questions about the physical universe. It develops theories of the world which best fit physically observed evidence. All scientific knowledge is probabilistic and subject to later improvement or revision in the face of better evidence. Scientific theories that have an overwhelming preponderance of favorable evidence are often treated as facts (such as the theories of gravity or evolution).

Many theories exist as to why religions sometimes seem to conflict with scientific knowledge. In the case of Christianity, a relevant factor may be that it was among Christians that science in the modern sense was developed. Unlike other religious groups, as early as the 17th century the Christian churches had to deal directly with this new way to investigate nature and seek truth. The perceived conflict between science and Christianity may also be partially explained by a literal interpretation of the Bible adhered to by many Christians, both currently and historically. This way of comprehending the sacred texts became especially prevalent after the rise of the Protestant reformation, with its emphasis on the Bible as the only authoritative source concerning the ultimate reality.

Some Christians have disagreed or are still disagreeing with scientists in areas such as the validity of Keplerian astronomy, the theory of evolution, the method of creation of the universe and the Earth, and the origins of life. On the other hand, scholars such as Stanley Jaki have suggested that Christianity and its particular worldview was a crucial factor for the emergence of modern science. In fact, most of today's historians are moving away from the view of the relationship between Christianity and science as one of "conflict" - a perspective commonly called the conflict thesis.Gary Ferngren in his historical volume about Science & Religion states:

> While some historians had always regarded the [conflict] thesis as oversimplifying and distorting a complex relationship, in the late twentieth century it underwent a more systematic re-evaluation. The result is the growing recognition among historians of science that the relationship of religion and science has been much more positive than is sometimes thought. Although popular images of controversy continue to exemplify the supposed hostility of Christianity to new scientific theories, studies have shown that Christianity has often nurtured and encouraged scientific endeavour, while at other times the two have co-existed without either tension or attempts at harmonization. If Galileo and the Scopes trial come to mind as examples of conflict, they were the exceptions rather than the rule. [1]

The philosophical approach known as pragmatism, as propounded by the American philosopher William James, has been used to reconcile scientific with religious knowledge. Pragmatism, simplistically, holds that the truth of a set of beliefs can be indicated by its usefulness in helping people cope with a particular context of life. Thus, the fact that scientific beliefs are useful in predicting observations in the physical world can indicate a certain truth for scientific theories; the fact that religious beliefs can be useful in helping people cope with difficult emotions or moral decisions can indicate a certain truth for those beliefs.

.

There is one consistent theme in all fields of human activity - the elicitation of the reality within, the discovery of external reality as well as the establishment of the relationship between the two -that strange two-way osmosis through the fragile membrane of our being. Science works from experiment to hypothesis and from hypothesis to falsification by experiment and so on, to fresh hypothesis; the successful hypothesis is successful, not because it informs, but because it works. In this sense pure science had grown nearer the applied. In religion, devotion appears more effective than enquiry; and because, by a quirk of human nature, we love our protégés better than our patrons, the emphasis of a church is on services; and faith is borne out in life, not because it has truth or error, but because it has conviction. While of course, in the arts, understanding comes more from the figments than the facts. In all it sometimes seems that it matters less to be right or wrong than to be sure.

We have made rapid strides in the field of science and technology including space exploration; we have left the scientific dimension of religion unexplored. These dimensions of the inner world, the hinterland of our own consciousness can alone unite us with our origin - the fountainhead of eternal bliss. The inner world of consciousness is terra incognita (unexplored region) to mankind. That is why the science of religion is the need of the hour. It is high time that religion is taught as a science of experience. The fact remains that in ethical religion, we impose restrictions and barriers of sorts. The so called custodians of religious have to accept the blame for hampering the individual growth aimed at entering the sphere of "Oneness" of all, irrespective of, color, creed, faith and nationality. The ethnical dimension is often guilty of nurturing sectarian and parochial feeling which is the greatest obstacle to achieving the goal of "one global family". This sectarian approach is highly responsible for numerous human maladies plaguing our world.

In seeking for truth, one needs to guard against the illusion that truths are definitive and mutually exclusive. The truth search is a never-ending enterprise. Truths evolve, and several truths can coexist. If we ever arrive the point where we think we thoroughly understand who we are and where we came from, life might lose much of its meaning. In pursuing the unfettered truth, we need to strip ourselves of false pretensions and all kinds of religious or scientific bigotry, cleanse our eyes, and prepare our minds to accept what our explorations tell us instead of trying to foister emotional predispositions on nature.

I believe that one of the prime causes of global religious fundamentalism and violent conflicts is the fact that the vast majority of us are yet to come to grips with the knowledge that all living things share a common ancestry through the process of evolution. Knowledge of our common origins can go a long way towards changing the way we perceive and treat each other. The next chapter examines the origin of living things.

2

The Origin of Life

Some call it evolution.
And others call it God.

- William Herbert Carruth (1841-1920).
  "Each in His Own Tongue"

How did life on earth originate? How will it end? Although we humans have undoubtedly asked these questions for as long as we've walked the earth, we've made spectacular progress on them in recent years. The Big Bang theory and Darwin's theory of Evolution are the pillars science uses to address the fundamental question of how we all got here. Let's take a closer look at each of these scientific theories:

The Big Bang

At the beginning of the 20th century, most scientists assumed a universe with no beginning and no end. Discoveries in astronomy and physics have however shown that our universe did in fact have a beginning. Prior to the world's beginning there was nothing; during and after that moment, there was something: our universe. Now pause for a moment and think about the miracle of this incredible event. Just try to imagine something popping out of thin air! *Ex-nihilo*! The big bang theory is an effort to explain what happened during and after that moment.

While most scientists don't believe in the concept of miracles, it is worth remembering that the big bang itself was a miracle. It is now commonly accepted that the universe began as a big bang that happened roughly 14 billion years ago. Undeniable evidence for the correctness of this theory was documented rather fortuitously by Arno Penzias and Robert Wilkson who in 1965 detected what appeared to be an annoying background of microwave signals regardless of where they pointed their new detector. After ruling out all other possible causes, Penzias and Wilson ultimately realized that this background noise was coming from the universe itself, and that it represented precisely the kind of afterglow that would be expected as a consequence of the Big Bang, arising from the annihilation of matter and antimatter in the early moments of the exploding universe. Further compelling evidence for the correctness of the Big Bang theory has been provided by the ratio of certain elements throughout the universe, principally hydrogen, deuterium, and helium. The abundance of deuterium is remarkably constant, from nearby stars to the farthest-flung galaxies near our event horizon. That finding suggests that all of the universe's deuterium was formed at extremely high temperatures in a single event during the Big Bang. If there were multiple such events in different locations and times, we would not expect such uniformity.

Based on these and other observations, physicists are in agreement that the universe began as an infinitely dense, dimensionless point of pure energy. The laws of physics don't apply in this circumstance, referred to as a "singularity". What is a "singularity" and where does it come from? No one knows for sure. Singularities are zones which defy our current understanding of physics. They are thought to exist at the core of "black holes." Black holes are areas of intense gravitational pressure. The pressure is thought to be so intense that finite matter is actually squished into infinite density (a mathematical concept which truly boggles the mind). These zones of infinite density are called "singularities." Our universe is thought to have begun as an infinitesimally small, infinitely hot, and infinitely dense something called a singularity. Where did it come from? We don't know. Why did it appear? No one knows. At least so far, scientists have been able to interpret the very earliest events in the explosion, occupying the first 10^{-43} seconds (one tenth of a millionth of a millionth of a millionth of a millionth of a millionth of a millionth of a second!).

After that, it is possible to make predictions about the events that would need to have occurred to result in today's observable universe, including the annihilation of matter and antimatter, the formation of stable atomic nuclei, and ultimately the formation of atoms, primarily hydrogen, deuterium and helium.

Scientists don't yet know whether the universe will keep expanding forever, or whether at some point gravitation will take over and the galaxies will begin to fall back together, ultimately resulting in a catastrophic "Big Crunch". What about the rest of creation? What are we to make of the long, drawn-out process by which our own planet, Earth, came into existence some 10 billion years after the Big bang? These questions belong to the realm of cosmology.

Cosmology and the Meaning of Life

When gazing up on a clear night, it's easy to feel small and insignificant due to the vastness of the firmament with all its splendor and majesty. The formation of the solar systems is commonly referred to as astronomical evolution. It's important to understand that evolution just means "developmental change over time," and to recognize the major differences between four types of proposed developments - in astronomical evolution (to form stars and galaxies, planets and solar systems), geological evolution (to form the earth's features), chemical evolution (to form the first life), and biological evolution (to form the diversity and complexity of life), which involve four very different sets of questions and observations.

For the first million years after the Big Bang, the universe expanded rapidly. This rapid expansion caused the temperature to drop, and nuclei and atoms of elements began to form. Matter began to coalesce into galaxies under the force of gravity, acquiring rotational motion as it did so, eventually resulting in the spiral shape of galaxies such as our own. Within those galaxies local collections of hydrogen and helium were drawn together, and their density and temperature rose in due course resulting in nuclear fusion, a process in which four hydrogen nuclei fuse together to form helium nucleus with release of vast amounts of energy. Nuclear fusion is the source of energy for the stars. Larger stars burn faster, producing within their core even heavier elements such as carbon and oxygen. Within the first few hundred million years, such elements appeared only in the core of these collapsing stars, but some of these stars then went through massive explosions known as supernovae, flinging heavier elements back into the gas in the galaxy. The stars we see in the night sky are part of a concentration of stars that we now call the Milky Way Galaxy, one with a specific shape and specific center. There are a vast number of stars within our galaxy (about 400 billion stars) of which the Sun is one.

Scientists are convinced our own sun did not form in the early days after the Big Bang; our sun is instead a second-or third-generation star, formed about 5 billion years ago by a local re-coalescence. As that was happening, a small proportion of heavier elements in the vicinity escaped absorption into the new star. Known as interstellar dust these heavier elements instead collected into the planets that now rotate around our sun. It is in dense concentrations of this dark interstellar material that new stars and new planetary systems are in the process of being born. This includes our own planet, which was far from friendly in its early days. Initially very hot, and bombarded with continual massive collisions, Earth gradually cooled, developed an atmosphere, and became potentially hospitable to living things about 4 billion years ago. A mere 150 million years later, the earth was teeming with life. Therefore we are all made up of stardust!

So how will it all end? Scientists have estimated that in some 5 or 6 or 7 billion years from now, the sun will become a red giant star and will engulf the orbits of Mercury and Venus and probably the Earth. The Earth then would be inside the Sun, and some of the problems that face us on this particular day will appear by comparison, modest. However, since it is still thousands of million years away, it is not our most pressing problem. But it is something to bear in mind because it has theological implications. Prior to Galileo discovery that the earth was not at the center of the solar system, theologians had long asserted otherwise. Now we know that our universe is just one of multiple universes in the cosmos.

Multiple Universes

Is physical reality larger than the part we can observe? Philosophers have long questioned whether there is in fact a real world out there, or whether "reality" is just a figment of our imagination. Then along came the quantum physicists, who unveiled an Alice-in-Wonderland realm of atomic uncertainty, where particles can be waves and solid objects dissolve away into ghostly patterns of quantum energy. Now cosmologists have gotten in on the act, suggesting that what we perceive as the universe might in fact be nothing more than a gigantic simulation. The story behind this bizarre suggestion began with a vexatious question: why is the universe so bio-friendly? Cosmologists have long been perplexed by the fact that the laws of nature seem to be cunningly concocted to enable life to emerge. Take the element carbon, the vital stuff that is the basis of all life. It wasn't made in the big bang that gave birth to the universe. Instead, carbon has been cooked in the innards of giant stars, which then exploded and spewed soot around the universe. The process that generates carbon is a delicate nuclear reaction. If the force that holds atomic nuclei together were just a tiny bit stronger or a tiny bit weaker, the reaction wouldn't work properly and life may never have happened.

The late British astronomer Fred Hoyle was so struck by the coincidence that the nuclear force possessed just the right strength to make beings like Fred Hoyle; he proclaimed the universe to be "a put-up job". Since this sounds a bit too much like divine providence, cosmologists have been scrambling to find a scientific answer to the conundrum of cosmic bio-friendliness. The theory they have come up with is multiple universes, or "the multiverse". This theory says that what we have been calling "the universe" is nothing of the sort. Rather, it is an infinitesimal fragment of a much grander and more elaborate system in which our cosmic region, vast though it is, represents but a single bubble of space amid a countless number of other bubbles, or pocket universes. Things get interesting when the multiverse theory is combined with ideas from sub-atomic particle physics. Evidence is mounting that what physicists took to be God-given unshakeable laws may be more like local by-laws, valid in our particular cosmic patch, but different in other pocket universes. Travel a trillion light years beyond the Andromeda galaxy, and you might find yourself in a universe where gravity is a bit stronger or electrons a bit heavier.

The vast majority of these other universes will not have the necessary fine-tuned coincidences needed for life to emerge; they are sterile and so go unseen. Only in Goldilocks universes like ours where things have fallen out just right, purely by accident, will sentient beings arise to be amazed at how ingeniously bio-friendly their universe is. It's a pretty neat idea, and very popular with scientists. But it carries a bizarre implication. Because the total number of pocket universes is unlimited, there are bound to be at least some that are not only inhabited, but populated by advanced civilizations - technological communities with enough computer power to create artificial consciousness. Indeed, some computer scientists think our technology may be on the verge of achieving thinking machines. So how can we judge whether intelligence is a likely evolutionary development or not? Simple: by searching for clues of intelligent life elsewhere in the vast cosmos. How rare are we? How unlikely? Does life exist elsewhere in the universe of the sort that we would recognize?

Intelligent Aliens

Some people believe that our maker may be an intelligent designer from outer space. This controversial hypothesis has been the subject of much heated speculation and debate. The search for Extraterrestrial Intelligence (SETI) Institute, begun by Francis Drake has now engaged physicists, astronomers and others in an organized effort to seek signals that might be coming from other civilizations in our galaxy.

What would be the potential theological implication of the discovery of life on other planets, should that come to pass? Would that event automatically render humankind on planet Earth less "special"? Would these extra-terrestrial cousins possess religions and worship the same God as we do? It is highly unlikely that any of us will have the opportunity to learn the answers to these questions during our lifetime.

We just reviewed the process by which the physical universe was created through the process of astronomical evolution. Let us now turn our attention to the formation of living things through the process of biological evolution and natural selection.

Evolution and Natural Selection*

Evolution by natural selection, the central concept of the life's work of Charles Darwin, is a theory. It's a theory about the origin of adaptation, complexity, and diversity among Earth's living creatures. It's such a dangerously wonderful and far-reaching view of life that some people find it unacceptable, despite the vast body of supporting evidence. As applied to our own species, *Homo sapiens,* it can seem more threatening still. Many fundamentalist Christians and ultra-orthodox Jews take alarm at the thought that human descent from earlier primates contradicts a strict reading of the Book of Genesis.

Their discomfort is paralleled by Islamic creationists such as Harun Yahya, author of a recent volume titled *The Evolution Deceit,* who points to the six-day creation story in the Koran as literal truth and calls the theory of evolution "nothing but a deception imposed on us by the dominators of the world system." The late Srila Prabhupada, of the Hare Krishna movement, explained that God created "the 8,400,000 species of life from the very beginning," in order to establish multiple tiers of reincarnation for rising souls. Although souls ascend, the species themselves don't change, he insisted, dismissing Darwin's nonsensical theory."

Others, not just scriptural literalists, remain unconvinced about evolution. According to a Gallup poll drawn from more than a thousand telephone interviews conducted in February 2001, no less than 45 percent of responding U.S. adults agreed that "God created human beings pretty much in their present form at one time within the last 10,000 years or so." Evolution, according to these people, played no role in shaping us.

---

*Excerpts from *Was Darwin Wrong,* article by David Quammen; NGM November 2004 V 206, no 5, adapted under license from National Geographic Magazine. Copyright reserved.

Only 37 percent of the polled Americans were satisfied with allowing room for both God and Darwin - that is, divine initiative to get things started, and evolution as the creative means. (This view, according to more than one papal pronouncement, is compatible with Roman Catholic dogma.) Still fewer Americans, only 12 percent, believed that humans evolved from other life-forms without any involvement of a god. The most startling thing about
these poll numbers is not that so many Americans reject evolution, but that the statistical breakdown hasn't changed much in two decades. Gallup interviewers posed exactly the same choices in 1982, 1993, 1997, and 1999. The creationist conviction - that God alone, and not evolution, produced humans - has never drawn less than 44 percent. In other words, nearly half the American populace prefers to believe that Charles Darwin was wrong where it mattered most.

Why are there so many antievolutionists? Scriptural literalism can only be part of the answer. The American public certainly includes a large segment of scriptural literalists - but not *that* large, not 44 percent. Creationist proselytizers and political activists, working hard to interfere with the teaching of evolutionary biology in public schools, are another part. Honest confusion and ignorance, among millions of adult Americans, must be still another. Many people have never taken a biology course that dealt with evolution nor read a book in which the theory was lucidly explained. Sure, we've all heard of Charles Darwin, and of a vague, somber notion about struggle and survival that sometimes goes by the catchall label "Darwinism." But the main sources of information from which most Americans have
drawn their awareness of this subject, it seems, are haphazard ones at best: cultural osmosis, newspaper and magazine references, half-baked nature documentaries on the television, and hearsay. Now, what is the truth about biological evolution?

Biological evolution in simple terms is descent with modification. This definition encompasses small-scale evolution (changes in gene frequency in a population from one generation to the next) and large-scale evolution (the descent of different species from a common ancestor over many generations). Evolution helps us to understand the history of life. Biological evolution is not simply a matter of change over time. Lots of things change over time: trees lose their leaves, mountain ranges rise and erode, but they aren't examples of biological evolution because they don't involve descent through genetic inheritance. The central idea of biological evolution is that all life on Earth shares a common ancestor, just as you and your cousins share a common grandmother. Through the process of descent with modification, the common ancestor of life on Earth gave rise to the fantastic diversity that we see documented in the fossil record and around us today. Evolution means that we're all distant cousins: humans and oak trees, hummingbirds and whales.

Evolution is both a beautiful concept and an important one, more crucial nowadays to human welfare, to medical science, and to our understanding of the world than ever before. It's also deeply persuasive - a theory you can take to the bank. Its main foundations are slightly more complicated than most people assume, but not so complicated that they can't be comprehended by any attentive person. Furthermore, the supporting evidence is abundant, various, ever increasing, solidly interconnected, and easily available in museums, popular books, textbooks, and a mountainous accumulation of peer-reviewed scientific studies. No one needs to, and no one should, accept evolution merely as a matter of faith. One of the fathers of the "modern synthesis" of evolutionary biology, Theodosius Dobzhansky, stated that "nothing in biology makes sense, except in the light of evolution." His words are equally true when applied to related fields, such as agriculture, medicine, and environmental and conservation biology.

The precise mechanisms which drive the evolution of species are still hotly debated. The current consensus is that primitive life evolved on earth about 3.5 billion years ago in the form of bacteria; they left behind traces of fossilized remains. Primitive plants subsequently evolved from the bacteria. A little over 1 billion years ago, small primitive animals emerged. They are absent from the fossil record because they lacked hard bodies and were not preserved in rock. The Cambrian period, (sometimes called the Cambrian explosion), began about 550 million years ago. Newly evolved species had developed hard bodies by this time, were preserved as fossils, and appear abundantly in the fossil record. Dinosaurs first appeared about 200 million years ago and died off at the end of the Cretaceous period, 64 million years ago. Mammals evolved from little four legged creatures during the end of the dinosaur era into about 4,000 species today, including humans.

Two big ideas, not just one, are at issue: the evolution of all species, as a historical phenomenon, and natural selection, as the main mechanism behind that phenomenon. Long before Darwin published *The Origin of Species* in 1859, the idea that all species are descended from common ancestors had been suggested by other thinkers, including Jean-Baptiste Lamarck, What made Darwin's book so remarkable when it appeared, and so influential in the long run, was that it offered a coherent explanation of how evolution must occur. The same insight came independently to Alfred Russell Wallace, a young naturalist doing fieldwork in the Malay Archipelago during the late 1850s. In historical annals, if not in the popular awareness, Wallace and Darwin share the kudos for having discovered natural selection.

The general idea of the concept is that small, random, heritable differences among individuals result in different chances of survival and reproduction - success for some, death without offspring for others, and that this natural culling leads to significant changes in shape, size, strength, armament, color, biochemistry, and behavior among the descendants. Excess population growth drives the competitive struggle. Because less successful competitors produce fewer surviving offspring, the useless or negative variations tend to disappear, whereas the useful variations tend to be perpetuated and gradually magnified throughout a population. Having examined anagenesis, during which a single species is transformed, let us now look at speciation.

Genetic changes sometimes accrue within an isolated segment of a species, but not throughout the whole, as that isolated population adapts to its local conditions. Gradually it goes its own way, seizing a new ecological niche. At a certain point it becomes irreversibly distinct, that is, so different that its members can't interbreed with the rest. Two species now exist where formerly there was one. Darwin called that splitting-and-specializing phenomenon the "principle of divergence." It was an important part of his theory, explaining the overall diversity of life as well as the adaptation of individual species.

This thrilling and radical assemblage of concepts came from an unlikely source. Charles Darwin was shy and meticulous, a wealthy landowner with close friends among the Anglican clergy. He had a gentle, unassuming manner, a strong need for privacy, and an extraordinary commitment to intellectual honesty. As an undergraduate at Cambridge, he had studied halfheartedly toward becoming a clergyman himself, before he discovered his real vocation as a scientist. Later, having established a good but conventional reputation in natural history, he spent 22 years secretly gathering evidence and pondering arguments - both for and against his theory, because he didn't want to flame out in a burst of unpersuasive notoriety. He may have delayed, too, because of his anxiety about announcing a theory that seemed to challenge conventional religious beliefs - in particular, the Christian beliefs of his wife, Emma. Darwin himself quietly renounced Christianity during his middle age, and later described himself as an agnostic. He continued to believe in a distant, impersonal deity of some sort, a greater entity that had set the universe and its laws into motion, but not in a personal God who had chosen humanity as a specially favored species. Darwin avoided flaunting his lack of religious faith, at least partly in deference to Emma. And she prayed for his soul. In 1859 he finally delivered his revolutionary book. Although it was hefty and substantive at 490 pages, he considered *The Origin of Species* just a quick-and-dirty "abstract" of the huge volume he had been working on until interrupted by an alarming event. (In fact, he'd wanted to title it *An Abstract of an Essay on the Origin of Species and Varieties through Natural Selection,* but his publisher found that insufficiently catchy.) The alarming event was his receiving a letter and an enclosed manuscript from Alfred Wallace, whom he knew only as a distant pen pal. Wallace's manuscript sketched out the same great idea - evolution by natural selection, that Darwin considered his own. Wallace had scribbled this paper and (unaware of Darwin's own evolutionary thinking, which so far had been kept private) mailed it to him from the Malay Archipelago, along with a request for reaction and help. Darwin was horrified. After two decades of painstaking effort, now he'd be scooped; or maybe not quite. He forwarded Wallace's paper toward publication, though managing also to assert his own prior claim by releasing two excerpts from his unpublished work. Then he dashed off *The Origin,* his "abstract" on the subject. Unlike Wallace, who was younger and less meticulous, Darwin recognized the importance of providing an edifice of supporting evidence and logic.

The evidence, as he presented it, mostly fell within four categories: biogeography, paleontology, embryology, and morphology. Biogeography is the study of the geographical distribution of living creatures, that is, which species inhabit which parts of the planet and why. Paleontology investigates extinct life-forms, as revealed in the fossil record. Embryology examines the revealing stages of development (echoing earlier stages of evolutionary history) that embryos pass through before birth or hatching; at a stretch, embryology also concerns the immature forms of animals that metamorphose, such as the larvae of insects. Morphology is the science of anatomical shape and design. Darwin devoted sizable sections of *The Origin of Species* to these categories.

Biogeography, for instance, offered a great pageant of peculiar facts and patterns. Anyone who considers the bio-geographical data, Darwin wrote, must be struck by the mysterious clustering pattern among what he called "closely allied" species - that is, similar creatures sharing roughly the same body plan. Such closely allied species tend to be found on the same continent (several species of zebras in Africa) or within the same group of oceanic islands (dozens of species of honeycreepers in Hawaii, 13 species of Galapagos finch), despite their species-by-species preferences for different habitats, food sources, or conditions of climate. Adjacent areas of South America, Darwin noted, are occupied by two similar species of large, flightless birds (the rheas, *Rhea americana* and *Pterocnemia pennata),* not by ostriches as in Africa or emus as in Australia. South America also has agoutis and

30

viscachas (small rodents) in terrestrial habitats, plus coypus and capybaras in the wetlands, not as Darwin wrote; hares and rabbits in terrestrial habitats or beavers and muskrats in the wetlands. During his own youthful visit to the Galapagos, aboard the survey ship *Beagle,* Darwin himself had discovered three very similar forms of mockingbird, each on a different island.

Why should "closely allied" species inhabit neighboring patches of habitat? And why should similar habitat on different continents be occupied by species that aren't so closely allied? "We see in these facts some deep organic bond, prevailing throughout space and time," Darwin wrote. "This bond, on my theory, is simply inheritance." Similar species occur nearby in space because they have descended from common ancestors.

Paleontology reveals a similar clustering pattern in the dimension of time. The vertical column of geologic strata, laid down by sedimentary processes over the eons, lightly peppered with fossils, represents a tangible record showing which species lived when. Less ancient layers of rock lie atop more ancient ones (except where geologic forces have tipped or shuffled them), and likewise with the animal and plant fossils that the strata contain. What Darwin noticed about this record is that closely allied species tend to be found adjacent to one another in successive strata. One species endures for millions of years and then makes its last appearance in, say, the middle Eocene epoch; just above, a similar but not identical species replaces it. In North America, for example, a vaguely horse like creature known as *Hyracotherium* was succeeded by *Orohippus,* then *Epihippus,* then *Mesohippus,* which in turn were succeeded by a variety of horsey American critters. Some of them even galloped across the Bering land bridge into Asia, then onward to Europe and Africa. By five million years ago they had nearly all disappeared, leaving behind *Dinohippus,* which was succeeded by *Equus,* the modern genus of horse. Not all these fossil links had been unearthed in Darwin's day, but he captured the essence of the matter anyway. Again, were such sequences just coincidental? No, Darwin argued. Closely allied species succeed one another in time, as well as living nearby in space, because they're related through evolutionary descent.

Embryology too involved patterns that couldn't be explained by coincidence. Why does the embryo of a mammal pass through stages resembling stages of the embryo of a reptile? Why is one of the larval forms of a barnacle, before metamorphosis, so similar to the larval form of a shrimp? Why the larvae of moths do, flies, and beetles resemble one another more than any of them resemble their respective adults? Because, Darwin wrote, "the embryo is the animal in its less modified state" and that state "reveals the structure of its progenitor."

Morphology, his fourth category of evidence, was the "very soul" of natural history, according to Darwin. Even today it's on display in the layout and organization of any zoo. Here are the monkeys, there are the big cats, and in that building are the alligators and crocodiles. Birds in the aviary, fish in the aquarium. Living creatures can be easily sorted into a hierarchy of categories - not just species but genera, families, orders, whole kingdoms, based on which anatomical characters they share and which they don't.

All vertebrate animals have backbones. Among vertebrates, birds have feathers, whereas reptiles have scales. Mammals have fur and mammary glands, not feathers or scales. Among mammals, some have pouches in which they nurse their tiny young. Among these species, the marsupials some have huge rear legs and strong tails by which they go hopping across miles of arid outback; we call them kangaroos. Bring in modern microscopic and molecular evidence, and you can trace the similarities still further back. All plants and fungi, as well as animals, have nuclei within their cells. All living organisms contain DNA and RNA (except some viruses with RNA only), two related forms of information-coding molecules.

Such a pattern of tiered resemblances - groups of similar species nested within broader groupings and all descending from a single source, isn't naturally present among other collections of items. You won't find anything equivalent if you try to categorize rocks, or musical instruments, or jewelry. Why not? Because rock types and styles of jewelry don't reflect unbroken descent from common ancestors. Biological diversity does. The number of shared characteristics between any one species and another indicates how recently those two species have diverged from a shared lineage.

That insight gave new meaning to the task of taxonomic classification, which had been founded in its modern form back in 1735 by the Swedish naturalist Carolus Linnaeus. Linnaeus showed how species could be systematically classified, according to their shared similarities, but he worked from creationist assumptions that offered no material explanation for the nested pattern he found. In the early and middle 19th century, morphologists such as Georges Cuvier and Étienne Geoffroy Saint-Hilaire in France and Richard Owen in England improved classification with their meticulous studies of internal as well as external anatomies, and tried to make sense of what the ultimate source of these patterned similarities could be. Not even Owen, a contemporary and onetime friend of Darwin's (later in life they had a bitter falling out), took the full step to an evolutionary vision before *The Origin of Species* was published. Owen made a major contribution, though, by advancing the concept of homologues - that is, superficially different but fundamentally similar versions of a single organ or trait, shared by dissimilar species.

For instance, the five-digit skeletal structure of the vertebrate hand appears not just in humans and apes and raccoons and bears but also, variously modified, in cats and bats and porpoises and lizards and turtles. The paired bones of our lower leg, the tibia and the fibula, are also represented by homologous bones in other mammals and in reptiles, and even in the long-extinct bird-reptile *Archaeopteryx*. What's the reason behind such varied recurrence of a few basic designs? Darwin, with a nod to Owen's "most interesting work," supplied the answer: common descent, as shaped by natural selection, modifying the inherited basics for different circumstances.

Vestigial characteristics are still another form of morphological evidence, illuminating to contemplate because they show that the living world is full of small, tolerable imperfections. Why do male mammals (including human males) have nipples? Why do some snakes (notably boa constrictors) carry the rudiments of a pelvis and tiny legs buried inside their sleek profiles? Why do certain species of flightless beetle have wings, sealed beneath wing covers that never open? Darwin raised all these questions, and answered them, in *The Origin of Species.* Vestigial structures stand as remnants of the evolutionary history of a lineage.

Today the same four branches of biological science from which Darwin drew - biogeography, paleontology, embryology, morphology - embrace an ever growing body of supporting data. In addition to those categories we now have others: population genetics, biochemistry, molecular biology, and, most recently, the whiz-bang field of machine-driven genetic sequencing known as genomics. These new forms of knowledge overlap one another seamlessly and intersect with the older forms, strengthening the whole edifice, contributing further to the certainty that Darwin was right.

He was right about evolution, that is. He wasn't right about *everything.* Being a restless explainer, Darwin floated a number of theoretical notions during his long working life, some of which were mistaken and illusory. He was wrong about what causes variation within a species. He was wrong about a famous geologic mystery, the parallel shelves along a Scottish valley called Glen Roy. Most notably, his theory of inheritance - which he labeled pangenesis and cherished despite its poor reception among his biologist colleagues - turned out to be dead wrong. Fortunately for Darwin, the correctness of his most famous good idea stood independent of that particular bad idea. Evolution by natural selection represented Darwin at his best - which is to say, scientific observation and careful thinking at its best.

Among most forms of living creatures, evolution proceeds slowly - too slowly to be observed by a single scientist within a research lifetime. But science functions by inference, not just by direct observation, and the inferential sorts of evidence such as paleontology and biogeography are no less cogent simply because they're indirect. Still, skeptics of evolutionary theory ask: Can we see evolution in action?

Can it be observed in the wild? Can it be measured in the laboratory? The answer is yes.

Peter and Rosemary Grant, two British-born researchers who have spent decades where Charles Darwin spent weeks, have captured a glimpse of evolution with their long-term studies of beak size among Galapagos finches. William R. Rice and George W. Salt achieved something similar in their lab, through an experiment involving 35 generations of the fruit fly *Drosophila melanogaster.* Richard E. Lenski and his colleagues at Michigan State University have done it too, tracking 20,000 generations of evolution in the bacterium *Escherichia coli.* Such field studies and lab experiments document anagenesis - that is, slow evolutionary change within a single, unsplit lineage. With patience it can be seen, like the movement of a minute hand on a clock.

Speciation, when a lineage splits into two species, is the other major phase of evolutionary change, making possible the divergence between lineages about which Darwin wrote. It's rarer and more elusive even than anagenesis. Many individual mutations must accumulate (in most cases, anyway, with certain exceptions among plants) before two populations become irrevocably separated. The process is spread across thousands of generations, yet it may finish abruptly - like a door going slam!, when the last critical changes occur. Therefore it's much harder to witness. Despite the difficulties, Rice and Salt seem to have recorded a speciation event, or very nearly so, in their extended experiment on fruit flies. From a small stock of mated females they eventually produced two distinct fly populations adapted to different habitat conditions, which the researchers judged "incipient species."

Studies of human variation, together with the fossil record, all point to an origin of modern humans approximately a hundred thousand years ago, most likely in East Africa. Genetic analyses suggest that approximately ten thousand ancestors gave rise to the entire population of 6 billion humans on the planet.

What about God?

Any discussion of the Big Bang theory and Evolution would be incomplete without asking the question, what about God? This is because cosmogony (the study of the origin of the universe) is an area where science and theology meet. Creation was a supernatural event. That is, it took place outside of the natural realm. This fact begs the question: is there anything else which exists outside of the natural realm? Specifically, is there a master Architect out there? We know that this universe had a beginning. Was God the "First Cause"?

3

Evolution and Religion

The beginning possibility of unification of religion and science is the most significant and exciting happening in our intellectual life today.

- Scott Peck, "The Road Less Traveled"

For many people of various faiths, support for the scientific theory of evolution has not supplanted their religious belief. And throughout the modern Judeo-Christian tradition, leaders have asserted that evolutionary science offers a valid perspective on the natural world. They say that evolution is consistent with religious doctrine and complements, rather than conflicts with, religion. There are, however, some Christians - in particular, fundamentalists and some evangelicals - who perceive a conflict between evolution and their literal interpretation of the Bible. Although all Christians base their beliefs on the teachings of Jesus, St. Paul, etc., they differ greatly in their fundamental understanding of the Bible. Some commentators assert that conservative and liberal Christians have diverged so greatly that they follow two very different spiritual paths - often viewed as two different religions who share the same name and Bible. These different perspectives are categorized as Theistic Evolutionists, Fundamentalists and other Evangelical Christians, Protestants Denominations as well as Roman Catholics.

Theistic Evolution

A theory of theistic evolution (also called evolutionary creation) proposes that God's method of creation was to cleverly design a universe in which everything would naturally evolve. Many Christian scientists find favor with this view. Theistic evolution (with God actively involved) differs from Einstein's *deistic* evolution (with God setting nature in motion and then just letting it run).

Fundamentalists and other Evangelical Christians

A key belief system of these faith groups is their belief in the inerrancy of the Bible. Since Genesis 1 describes how God created the universe, and in a certain sequence, there is no doubt that he did exactly that. A debate exists with conservative Christianity over the length of each "day" in Genesis: i.e. whether the word "day" means an interval of 24 hours, or an era of indeterminate duration. Some theologians believe that the Hebrew word "yom" has multiple meanings in various locations in Genesis. A number of competing theories have been formulated by Christian creation scientists in an attempt to harmonize Genesis and the fossil record.

Most conservative Christians are particularly insistent on the literal truth of the creation stories in Genesis. If those passages were shown to be false, then the Garden of Eden story, the fall of humanity and the alienation between God and man would all be in doubt. Some feel that this could negate the need for Jesus' execution and resurrection. Some believe that the entire conservative Christian message would collapse like a deck of cards, if Genesis is shown to be a fable. One writer has said: "Overthrow Genesis and you destroy the whole foundation of Christianity. Evolution is just a modern version of the old Pelagian heresy. If Genesis is not historically accurate, then there was no Fall of man and no need for a Savior. Man is then free to exalt himself and even to take Christ's place on earth!!" [1]

Liberal Protestant Denominations

These churches have accepted and even promoted the theory of evolution for decades. Although there are many unresolved details about the evolution of species on earth and of the matter and energy in the rest of the universe, scientists have reached a consensus on the broad mechanisms of evolution. Most researchers agree that the universe originated at a "Big Bang" some 20 billion years ago. Some matter coalesced into stars of which our sun is one. The earth and other planets coalesced out of stellar material many billions of years ago. A few billion years in the past, the first elementary forms of life appeared; these evolved into the multiplicity of species that we see today, including humanity. By accepting evolution, liberal Christians have either: assigned symbolic meanings to the stages of creation in the two creation stories of Genesis 1 and 2, or treated those passages as creation myths, similar to the hundreds of creation stories from numerous other religions. Many Christian scientists find favor with this view.

Mainline Protestant Denominations

Many members and their religious organizations adopt either the positions of Evangelicals or that of liberal denominations. To some, evolution is not really a religious issue. Others have adopted theistic evolution (a.k.a. called "process creation", or "multiple creations"). In this belief system, God originally created the universe. Later, God used evolution as the technique by which new species develop. One example of a mainline Christian's view of evolution is seen in the writings of Kitty Ferguson: "How do we know when biblical writers intended to have their words interpreted literally and figuratively, when they were speaking in parables and when not?...The question how far we can accept the Bible as accurate historical evidence continues to be debated by responsible scholars, as well as by ideologues of both extremes, but very little gets settled." [2]

Roman Catholic Church

Pope Pius XII released an encyclical in 1950 titled "Humani Generis." It "considered the doctrine of 'evolutionism' as a serious hypothesis, worthy of a more deeply studied investigation and reflection on a par with the opposite hypothesis."[3] The encyclical states in part:

"For these reasons the Teaching Authority of the Church does not forbid that...research and discussions, take place with regard to the doctrine of evolution, in as far as it inquires into the origin of the human body as coming from pre-existent and living matter...However, this must be done in such a way that the reasons for both opinions, that is, those favorable and those unfavorable to evolution, be weighed and judged with the necessary seriousness, moderation and measure, and provided that all are prepared to submit to the judgment of the Church." [4]

The Second Vatican Council stated that the Bible is inerrant (free of any error) in those texts that contain religious truth that have been revealed for personal salvation. However, the implication is that the Bible is not necessarily free from error elsewhere - for example where it discusses scientific matters.

In 1996, Pope John Paul II spoke at the annual meeting of the Pontifical Academy of Sciences, which has been called "the Church's 'scientific senate' ". [5,6] He said, in part:

> "Today, more than a half century after this ['Humani Generis'] encyclical, new knowledge leads us to recognize in the theory of evolution more than a hypothesis. ... The convergence, neither sought nor induced, of results of work done independently one from the other, constitutes in itself a significant argument in favor of this theory [of evolution]." [7]

Walter Taminang

Limits of Darwin's Theory

Darwin's theory is irrefutable as far as it goes, but it is unable to explain by natural selection the growth of the senses that must, in their early stages, have been a hindrance to survival. It also fails to explain the characteristics that have nothing to do with capacities nor does it explain how the more advanced forms of life show an increasing proportion of 'mental' or 'spiritual' aptitudes indifferent, if not inimical to the physical defenses and protective mechanisms. Why does intelligence, which is inefficient, take over from instinct, which is efficient? That intelligence may be the better fitted to meet new challenges is to suggest a precognitive element in natural selection directed towards, not the genes of ancestry but the ghosts of posterity yet unborn. Does natural selection operate by pre-empting? Why do humans have personalities? A very strict interpretation of Darwinism gives no allowance for the continuing survival of people who have passed their procreative stage but still live on to share the common board and add to the burden of providing for them. Why has natural selection allowed quantities at cost to survive?

Natural selection is distinguished by its peculiar economy; an economy that is manifest in the finished products and exercised in ruthless extermination of the unfit. Nature may be lavish in her efforts but she is stingy of her output; she grows and prunes with equal zeal; and however widely she sows, so widely does she weed. Even the mating display of the peacock is wasteful of effect to make saving in effort; ostentatious but inexpensive; an extravagant show is a better way of catching a mate than chasing her. Higher animals have learnt the same lesson the hard way.

Life is growth; and evolution-the life of life-multiplies the anomalies which the individual contains. The long-term development of the senses often runs counter to the short-term effect of natural selection. While, as evolution moves from race survival to personal expression, the excellence of the individual takes precedence over the duration of the race, until survival, in the higher creatures, is less important than differentiation, and the qualities which persist beyond the mating are a

41

small abstraction from a life that seems lived for its own value. And in man, who breeds young and develops late, the latter development is of value to the person, not to the species.

One other paradox of evolution remains that science has not yet explained. The evolution of a sophisticated creature halted, not by the mere fact of the suitability of environment, but by a dying away of the power to mutate. At a certain stage in its evolution, it ceases to bid upon the market of natural selection. The machinery of evolution is subject to an unknown control; there is channeling of randomness. The creature may develop but not change; in effect, it is what is, and will meet the future pressures of natural selection by adaptation, not alteration.

When matter was first inspired (or was it cooked?) into life, the many half-attempts at viability were repeated and modified until successful. Such conditions of temperature, humidity, atmospheric content, will not be repeated unless, perhaps, towards earth's end. It seems that until the world's slow dying in a swollen sun, there will be no more chance of spontaneous generation; that only in the fervors of the world's infancy or the fevers of the world's ageing may new life arise-for whatever significance that fact may contain.

It is certainly a fact that the basic physical and chemical laws are almost startling in their simplicity; the immensity and subtlety of detail which follows from them are a mere usage of childlike opinions. Eddington's contention that all knowledge is basically *a priori* is, indeed, worth re-examining. For instance, it is possible that the theory of evolution could have been deduced from first principles in the complete absence of anthropological and physiological evidence by recognition that whatever god there is could not create man; he could only create the possibility of man; he could only furnish the opportunity. For man is growth, each person is the accumulation of his years; and because the part is analogous to the whole, it follows that every living species, with the accumulated instincts and capacities of its ancestry, is itself and the growing product of time and environment.

4.

Major World Religions

There is only one religion, though there are a hundred versions of it.

-   George Bernard Shaw

I believe that almost everyone has at one time or another pondered the multiplicity of religions in world, the conflicting truth- claims of the different religious traditions, as well as their doctrinal differences. If there is only one truth, why should the messages given by the different religions be so confusingly different? Why should there be so many revelations that do not agree with each other, and which all bear the hallmarks of the time and place of their conception? Are the present religions just a phase of a continuous evolution toward one universal religion?

Perhaps at no other time in history has it seemed more important to understand not only our own religions, but also those of others. What specifically, do the followers of the world's largest religions believe? How do they view those who do not share their understanding of God? Unfortunately, these questions - ones that can yield genuine understanding of how religions are lived and practiced - are rarely asked in contemporary discussions of religion, especially in the news media. Such questions are the focus of this chapter.

In summary, religious adherence of the world's population is as follows: "Abrahamic": 53.5%, "Indian": 19.7%, irreligious: 14.3%, "Far Eastern": 6.5%, tribal religions: 4.0%, new religious movements: 2.0%.Abrahamic religions are by far the largest group, and these consist primarily of Christianity, Islam, Judaism and sometimes Baháʼí is also included. [1] They are named for the patriarch Abraham, and are unified by their strict monotheism. Today, around 3.4 billion people are followers of Abrahamic religions and are spread widely around the world apart from the regions around South-East Asia. Several Abrahamic organizations are vigorous proselytizers. Indian religions originated in Greater India and tend to share a number of key concepts, such as dharma and karma. They are of the most influence across the Indian subcontinent, East Asia, South East Asia, as well as isolated parts of Russia. The main Indian religions are Hinduism, Buddhism, Sikhism, and Jainism. Indian religions mutually influenced each other. Sikhism was also influenced by the Abrahamic tradition of Sufism.

Far Eastern religions consist of several East Asian religions which make use of the concept of Tao (in Chinese) or Do (in Japanese or Korean). They include Taoism, Confucianism, Shinto, Chondogyo, Caodaism, and Yiguandao as well as Far Eastern Buddhism (in which the group overlaps with the "Indian" group). Indigenous tribal religions, formerly found on every continent, now marginalized by the major organized faiths, but persisting as undercurrents of folk religion: Includes African traditional religions, Asian Shamanism, Native American religions, Austronesian and Australian Aboriginal traditions and arguably Chinese folk religion (overlaps with Far Eastern religions).

New religious movements, a heterogeneous group of religious faiths emerging since the 19th century, often syncretizing, re-interpreting or reviving aspects of older traditions (Baháʼí, Hindu revivalism, Ayyavazhi, Pentecostalism, polytheistic reconstructionism), some inspired by science-fiction (UFO religions, Scientology).

The chart below depicts the major world religions.

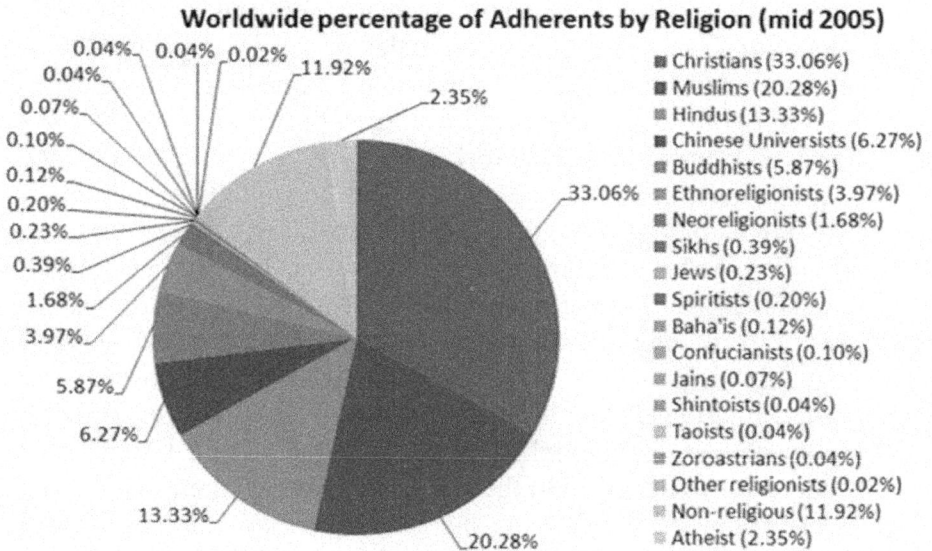

Worldwide percentage of Adherents by Religion (mid 2005)

0.04% 0.04% 0.02%
0.04%
0.07%
0.10%
0.12%
0.20%
0.23%
0.39%
1.68%
3.97%
5.87%
6.27%
13.33%
11.92%
2.35%
33.06%
20.28%

- Christians (33.06%)
- Muslims (20.28%)
- Hindus (13.33%)
- Chinese Universists (6.27%)
- Buddhists (5.87%)
- Ethnoreligionists (3.97%)
- Neoreligionists (1.68%)
- Sikhs (0.39%)
- Jews (0.23%)
- Spiritists (0.20%)
- Baha'is (0.12%)
- Confucianists (0.10%)
- Jains (0.07%)
- Shintoists (0.04%)
- Taoists (0.04%)
- Zoroastrians (0.04%)
- Other religionists (0.02%)
- Non-religious (11.92%)
- Atheist (2.35%)

Major religious groups as a percentage of the world population in 2005 (source: *Encyclopaedia Britannica*).

Christianity

We define as "Christian" any person or group who thoughtfully, sincerely, prayerfully regard themselves as Christian. This is the definition that pollsters and the census offices of many countries use. It includes as Christians the full range of faith groups who consider themselves to be Christians, including Assemblies of God members, Presbyterians, Roman Catholics, Southern Baptists, United Church members, Jehovah's Witnesses, Mormons, etc. Many Christians have a much less inclusive definition of the term "Christian." Christianity is a monotheistic and evangelistic faith that is centered on the life and teachings of Jesus Christ. Christianity is the largest world religion with 2.1 billion adherents. [2] Like Judaism and Islam, Christianity is an Abrahamic religion.Like its source, Judaism, Christianity evolved around the conviction of the possibility of a human relationship with a personal, caring, and just God who is also the omnipotent Creator of the universe. For Christians, this relationship is defined by the core belief that the divine became revealed in a unique, historic person, an itinerant Jewish preacher, *Yeshua Ben Joseph* or *Yeshua of Nazareth.* Later, Pauline Christians gave him the title *Jesus Christ* (*Jesus* was derived from *Iesous*, the Greek version of *Yeshua*; *Christ* means *Messiah*, the anointed one - a title often given to King of Israel). Roman Catholics, Evangelical Christians, many other Christians, and Muslims believe that his mother, Mary, was a virgin when he was conceived; her pregnancy was caused by the Holy Spirit, and did not result from human sexual intercourse. He was born in Palestine, a small Jewish territory in the vast Roman Empire, a loose amalgamation of countless nations, languages, cultures, religions, cults, and competing deities, probably circa 4 to 7 BCE. Some believe that his birth occurred in the springtime, during the time that the lambs were giving birth, when the shepherds were watching their flocks by night. He was raised by his Jewish family of origin in the city of Nazareth in the Galilee.

Yeshua was the eldest child in the family. The Bible refers to his four brothers by name and at least two sisters who were not considered important enough to name. (Some Christians believe that Mary had no further children, and regard these "brothers" as either step-siblings, cousins, or close friends). At the time, Palestine was very unstable politically. It had been under severe Roman oppression for decades. Many Jews expected the imminent arrival in Galilee of a military/political/religious leader, the *Messiah,* (Anointed One) who would lead them to a military victory over the occupation forces and later reign as king. This would be followed by the Reign of God on earth. The Zealots were actively promoting the overthrow of the Romans. At the age of about 30, circa 26 CE, he was baptized by John the Baptist, who was perhaps his cousin. John was a Jewish prophet, and probably a member of the Essenes. The Essenes were the smallest of the four largest Jewish religious/political groups active in Jerusalem at the time; the others being the Pharisees, Sadducees, and Zealots. Yeshua became an itinerant preacher whose message found an enthusiastic audience. He collected a group of followers during his ministry of which about 10 are fully described in the Christian Scriptures (New Testament); about half were male, and half female. (The Bible says that there were 12 disciples at one time and 70 at another. It has multiple lists of the twelve, but the names differ. Many Christians believe that he had exactly 12 disciples, all male, that women held a lower status among his followers, and that they were not eligible for consideration as disciples).

Jesus lived almost 2000 years ago at a time when divinity was understood primarily in terms of imperial power and demand for absolute obedience. Yeshua of Nazareth (a.k.a. Jesus Christ) conducted a short ministry (one year, in the Galillee according to the synoptic gospels; perhaps three years, mainly in Judea according to the Gospel of John). His teachings closely matched those of Beit Hillel (the House of Hillel). Hillel was a great Jewish rabbi who lived in the second half of the 1st century BCE one or two generations before Yeshua's birth. Jesus preached a message of radical love rooted in his experience of the Father as an implacably, passionately loving cosmic force, and that message is as relevant today as it was two millennia ago. The essence of Christianity, the living center, is that "radioactive" love that can purify, activate, and transform whatever it touches. Jesus challenges us not only to love family, friends, and associates, but to love our enemies. Jesus challenges us to turn the other cheek, to be kind to those who hurt us, to give to others without expecting anything in return, to go the extra mile. Jesus challenges us to overcome all innate tendencies we might have to hate or "get even," no matter how serious the provocation. He lived by his own principles to the end. As he hung on the cross he asked that his tormentors be forgiven. Jesus challenges us to be the best we can be and to remember that we are created in the image of God, called to actualize the divine spark within us. This call to the practice of radical love is the essence of Christianity, and it transcends all denominational boundaries. His preaching aroused the envy of some Jewish religious leaders and his popularity made him suspect among Roman authorities who routinely crucified political enemies and were always prepared to nip another Jewish insurrection in the bud.

The Gospels record a violent event in the Jewish Temple at Jerusalem, where Yeshua committed aggravated assault with a whip against shopkeepers. Some theologians believe that this was the incident that triggered his arrest and sentencing. He is recorded in the Christian Scriptures (New Testament) as being betrayed by Judas, one of his followers. He was executed in Jerusalem about Passover circa 30 CE by the Roman authorities. Jesus had promised that he would never leave his people. Three days after his burial, his tomb was found to be empty. His followers reported that they continued to see him alive, his resurrected body bearing the wounds of the crucifixion, and fifty days after his resurrection his followers were gathered together for the Jewish feast of Shavuos, a wheat harvest festival and a celebration of the giving of the Torah to Moses. Suddenly, as reported in the Book of Acts, the room was filled with a violent storm and tongues of fire leapt among them and they were filled with the Spirit of God, also called the Paraclete, who would give them the ability to share the message of their ascended Lord, the Good News of the Father's implacable love, with the world. Christians still celebrate that day annually as Pentecost, "The birthday of the Church."

This pivotal experience of their living, dying, and resurrected Lord became the kernel round which Christianity began to coalesce, first as one Jewish sect among others, and eventually in the form of a growing number of Christian house churches, sharing a family resemblance, and often under women leaders. Many of his followers expected that he will return shortly and initiate the Kingdom of God on earth. Thus, for Christians, Jesus is at once the primary way of relating to God and the world, the model to be emulated in life, and a way of imagining the Divine. The Christian is called to follow Jesus whose Hebrew name means "YHWH (Yahweh) is salvation." In other words, for Christians, Jesus of Nazareth--his manner of thinking, acting, and being--is the standard that informs (or should inform) life as it is lived in the present. The New Testament offers clues that can help us become such followers of Jesus but, because of the limitations of language and the cultural chasms that divide contemporary Christians from one another and the worlds of the past, we must never forget that, as Paul already realized, we always see in (or through) "a glass darkly" whether we speak of God or try to understand scripture. The glass could be the focusing/distorting lens of our interpretive faculties or the more or less uneven mirror of our minds. Either way, absolute certainty eludes us. Hence, it is not surprising that there is in practice not only one Christianity, there are thousands of Christianities, all of which claim to be genuine – and often exclusively true – ways of following Jesus and imagining the Divine.

Early Christendom

For the first three centuries after the death of Christ, the Romans tried to suppress Christianity, in part because Christian pacifism was considered an expression of disloyalty to the military ethos of the state. In 70 CE, the Romans destroyed the temple and the rest of Jerusalem. Many Jews were killed; others fled Palestine. After an unsuccessful Jewish uprising in the 130's, the Roman Army drove the Jews from Palestine. The Nazarenes were thus dispersed throughout the Roman Empire. This severely weakened the movement. They had a brief resurgence during the 2nd century CE, but then disappeared. Many were probably absorbed by the mainline Pauline Christian movement which grew out of the churches established by Paul and his coworkers. Ironically, in 313 Emperor Constantine legalized this new religion of peace because, according to tradition, he had won a major battle with the aid of the Christian God. Therefore, with his first obligations remaining to the empire, Constantine the emperor of Rome, himself a pagan and long persecutor of the Christians, declared himself a Christian and first Christian Emperor. He appointed himself leader and overseer of the Christians and Pagans alike. This singular incident marked a huge turning point in the history of Christianity. With astounding rapidity, the position of the Christians had reversed. Their persecution by Rome ended and Christians were now considered a "religiolicita", a licensed cult with equal status to the other religions. With their new status, the Christians had a right to profess their faith without fear of recrimination and legal impediments. They were free to regain property that had been confiscated during the period of their persecution. They hailed Constantine as the champion of their cause. It did not make Christianity the state religion as is generally asserted, but only legalized and popularized it, thus paving the way for the Catholic hierarchy and marking a new era in the history of the Christian church.

As time went on, Constantine portrayed himself as the God's appointed sovereign, rewarded with favor. This conversion and the merging of Christianity with Paganism stopped the persecution of Christians, but also brought with it many changes to the Christian faith. Emperor Constantine's involvement in deciding church doctrine aand practices is most readily seen in the events at the Council of Aries (A.D. 314) and the Council of Nicea (A.D. 324).

How the Christian "families" evolved:

With the exception of the first few years after the execution of their founder Yeshua of Nazareth (a.k.a. Jesus Christ), Christianity was never a unified religion. During the first six decades of the first century CE, Judaism was composed of about two dozen competing factions: Sadducees, Pharisees, Essenes, Zealots, followers of John the Baptist, followers of Yeshua of Nazareth (Iesous in Greek, Iesus in Latin, Jesus in English), followers of other charismatic leaders, etc. All followed common Jewish practices, such as observing dietary restrictions, worshiping at the Jerusalem temple, sacrificing animals, observing weekly sabbaths, etc. By the end of the 1st century CE three main movements remained:

Pauline Christians: a group of mainline congregations, largely of non-Jewish Christians. Some had been created by Paul and his co-workers. They evolved to become the established church.

Gnostic Christians: They claimed salvation through special, otherwise secret *gnosis* (knowledge). Some were members of mainline congregations; others were part of Gnostic groups. They were declared heretics and were gradually suppressed and exterminated.

Jewish Christians: remnants of the group originally headed by James, the brother of Yeshua, and including Jesus' disciples. They were scattered throughout the Roman Empire after the destruction of Jerusalem in 70 CE, and gradually disappeared.

Circa 400 CE: The Bishop of Rome began to be recognized as the most senior of all bishops. Siricius (384-399 CE) became the first bishop to be called Pope.

1054 CE: A lengthy power struggle between eastern and western Christianity culminated in a schism between the *Eastern Orthodox* churches and the *Western Rite* (later often called the Roman Catholic Church). Many Christian sects broke away from the Western Rite throughout the Middle Ages (*Cathars, Knights Templars,* etc.). These were generally exterminated by the central church in various genocidal wars.

1517 CE: Martin Luther attacked certain practices and beliefs of the Church, and the authority of the Pope. He was followed by other reformers which produced a mass movement -- the *Protestant Reformation.* They were driven largely by two fundamental principles: *"Sola Scriptura" (Scripture Alone)*: The belief that the Holy Bible was the ultimate authority for all matters of religious belief and practice. *The Priesthood of all Believers*: The belief that no priest or other intermediary is needed between the Christian believer and God.

1820: Joseph Smith, at the age of 14, received his first vision. He reported that God and Jesus Christ had appeared before him as separate entities and told him that all of the Christian sects and denominations were in error and that he should not join any of them. He founded *The Church of Jesus Christ of Latter-day Saints* in 1830. It attracted 1,000 members during its first 12 months and has since grown rapidly. About 13 million believers who are members of almost a hundred faith groups trace their church's history back to the church that Smith founded.

Into modern times

Protestant Christianity became fractured into over 1,500 individual denominations, as individuals and groups began to interpret the Bible in their own unique ways. They continually formed new sects that they felt were closer to Jesus' intentions for the church. In the past fifteen decades in North America schisms occurred over the legitimacy of human slavery, and whether to allow women to be ordained. A number of mainline denominations - Presbyterian, Methodist, Episcopal - are attempting to keep their organizations intact in spite of differences of belief about sexual orientation. They are debating whether to grant equal rights to gays and lesbians, and whether to recognize same-sex relationships.

Islam

Islam is a monotheistic Abrahamic religion originating with the teachings of Muhammad, a 7th century Arab religious and political figure. The word Islam means "submission", or the total surrender of oneself to God. An adherent of Islam is known as a Muslim, meaning "one who submits (to God)". There are approximately 1.61 billion Muslims, making Islam the second-largest religion in the world, after Christianity.

Muslims believe that God revealed the Qur'an to Muhammad, God's final prophet, and regard the Qur'an and the Sunnah (words and deeds of Muhammad) as the fundamental sources of Islam. They do not regard Muhammad as the founder of a new religion, but as the restorer of the original monotheistic faith of Abraham, Moses, Jesus, and other prophets. Islamic tradition holds that Jews and Christians distorted the texts God gave to these prophets by either altering the text, using a false interpretation, or both.

Islam includes many religious practices. Adherents are generally required to observe the Five Pillars of Islam, which are five duties that unite Muslims into a community. In addition to the Five Pillars, Islamic law (sharia) has developed a tradition of rulings that touch on virtually all aspects of life and society. This tradition encompasses everything from practical matters like dietary laws and banking to warfare.

Almost all Muslims belong to one of two major denominations, the Sunni and Shi'a. The schism developed in the late 7th century following disagreements over the religious and political leadership of the Muslim community. Roughly 85 percent of Muslims are Sunni and 15 percent are Shi'a. Islam is the predominant religion throughout the Middle East, as well as in parts of Africa and Asia. Large communities are also found in China, the Balkan Peninsula in Eastern Europe and Russia. There are also large Muslim immigrant communities in wealthier and more developed parts of the world such as Western Europe. About 20 percent of Muslims live in Arab countries.

Articles of faith

Muslims believe that God revealed his final message to humanity through the Islamic prophet Muhammad via the angel Gabriel. For them, Muhammad was God's final prophet and the Qur'an is the revelations he received over more than two decades. In Islam, prophets are men selected by God to be his messengers. Muslims believe that prophets are human and not divine, though some are able to perform miracles to prove their claim. Islamic prophets are considered to be the closest to perfection of all humans, and are uniquely the recipients of divine revelation—either directly from God or through angels. Islamic theology says that all of God's messengers since Adam preached the message of Islam—submission to the will of the one God. Islam is described in the Qur'an as "the primordial nature upon which God created mankind", and the Qur'an states that the proper name Muslim was given by Abraham.

Muhammad

Muhammad (c. 570 – July 6, 632) was an Arab religious, political, and military leader who founded the religion of Islam as a historical phenomenon. Muslims view him not as the creator of a new religion, but as the restorer of the original, uncorrupted monotheistic faith of Adam, Abraham and others. In Muslim tradition, Muhammad is viewed as the last and the greatest in a series of prophets—as the man closest to perfection, the possessor of all virtues. For the last 23 years of his life, beginning at age 40, Muhammad reported receiving revelations from God. The content of these revelations, known as the Qur'an, was memorized and recorded by his companions.
During this time, Muhammad preached to the people of Mecca,

53

imploring them to abandon polytheism. Although some converted to Islam, Muhammad and his followers were persecuted by the leading Meccan authorities. After 13 years of preaching, Muhammad and the Muslims performed the Hijra ("emigration") to the city of Medina (formerly known as Yathrib) in 622. There, with the Medinan converts (Ansar) and the Meccan migrants (Muhajirun), Muhammad established his political and religious authority. Within years, two battles had been fought against Meccan forces: the Battle of Badr in 624, which was a Muslim victory, and the Battle of Uhud in 625, which ended inconclusively. Conflict with Medinan Jewish clans who opposed the Muslims led to their exile, enslavement or death, and the Jewish enclave of Khaybar was subdued. At the same time, Meccan trade routes were cut off as Muhammad brought surrounding desert tribes under his control. By 629 Muhammad was victorious in the nearly bloodless Conquest of Mecca, and by the time of his death in 632 he ruled over the Arabian Peninsula. In Islam, the "normative" example of Muhammad's life is called the Sunnah (literally "trodden path"). This example is preserved in traditions known as hadith ("reports"), which recount his words, his actions, and his personal characteristics.

Duties and practices

Five Pillars of Islam

The Five Pillars of Islam (Arabic: اركان الدين) are five practices essential to Sunni Islam. Shi'a Muslims subscribe to eight ritual practices which substantially overlap with the Five Pillars. Now let us briefly examine each of these pillars.

The *Shahadah*, is the basic creed or tenet of Islam, "'ašhadu 'al-lā ilāha illā-llāhu wa 'ašhadu 'anna muḥammadan rasūlu-llāh", or "I testify that there is none worthy of worship except God and I testify that Muhammad is the Messenger of God." This testament is a foundation for all other beliefs and practices in Islam.

Salah, or ritual prayer, which must be performed five times a day. In many Muslim countries, reminders called Adhan (call to prayer) are broadcast publicly from local mosques at the appropriate times. The prayers are recited in the Arabic language, and consist of verses from the Qur'an.

Zakat, or alms-giving. This is the practice of giving based on accumulated wealth, and is obligatory for all Muslims who can afford it. A fixed portion is spent to help the poor or needy, and also to assist the spread of Islam.

Sawm, or fasting during the month of Ramadan. Muslims must not eat or drink (among other things) from dawn to dusk during this month, and must be mindful of other sins. The fast is to encourage a feeling of nearness to God, and during it Muslims should express their gratitude for and dependence on him, atone for their past sins, and think of the needy. Sawm is not obligatory for several groups for whom it would constitute an undue burden. For others, flexibility is allowed depending on circumstances, but missed fasts usually must be made up quickly.

The *Hajj*, or the pilgrimage during the Islamic month of *Dhu al-Hijjah* in the city of Mecca. Every able-bodied Muslim who can afford it must make the pilgrimage to Mecca at least once in his or her lifetime. In addition to the khums tax, Shi'a Muslims consider three additional practices essential to the religion of Islam. The first is jihad, which is also important to the Sunni, but not considered a pillar. The second is Amr-Bil-Ma'rūf ,the "Enjoining to Do Good", which calls for every Muslim to live a virtuous life and to encourage others to do the same. The third is Nahi-Anil-Munkar, the "Exhortation to Desist from Evil", which tells Muslims to refrain from vice and from evil actions and to also encourage others to do the same.

Law

The Sharia (literally: "the path leading to the watering place") is Islamic law formed by traditional Islamic scholarship. In Islam, Sharia is the expression of the divine will, and "constitutes a system of duties that are incumbent upon a Muslim by virtue of his religious belief". Islamic law covers all aspects of life, from matters of state, like governance and foreign relations, to issues of daily living. The Qur'an defines hudud as the punishments for five specific crimes: unlawful intercourse, false accusation of unlawful intercourse, consumption of alcohol, theft, and highway robbery. The Qur'an and Sunnah also contain laws of inheritance, marriage, and restitution for injuries and murder, as well as rules for fasting, charity, and prayer. However, these prescriptions and prohibitions may be broad, so their application in practice varies.

Religion and state

Islamic law does not distinguish between "matters of church" and "matters of state"; the ulema function as both jurists and theologians. In practice, Islamic rulers frequently bypassed the Sharia courts with a parallel system of so-called "Grievance courts" over which they had sole control. As the Muslim world came into contact with Western secular ideals, Muslim societies responded in different ways. Turkey has been governed as a secular state ever since the reforms of Mustafa Kemal Atatürk. In contrast, the 1979 Iranian Revolution replaced a mostly secular regime with an Islamic republic led by the Ayatollah Ruholla Khomeini.

Jihad

Islamic term, Arabic for 'battle; struggle; holy war for the religion', and is considered the "sixth pillar of Islam" by a minority of Muslim authorities.[3] Jihad has two possible definitions: the greater, which is the spiritual struggle of each man, against vice, passion and ignorance. This understanding of jihad has been presented by apologetics of modern times, but is an understanding of the term rarely used by Muslims themselves. The lesser jihad is simplified to cover holy war against infidels and infidel countries, aiming at spreading Islam. This kind of jihad is described in both the Koran and in the hadiths. Jihad, in its broadest sense, is classically defined as "exerting one's utmost power, efforts, endeavors, or ability in contending with an object of disapprobation." Depending on the object being a visible enemy, the devil, and aspects of one's own self, different categories of Jihad are defined. Jihad when used without any qualifier is understood in its military aspect.

Divisions of Islam

Islam consists of a number of religious denominations that are essentially similar in belief but which have significant theological and legal differences. The primary division is between the Sunni and the Shi'a, with Sufism generally considered to be a mystical inflection of Islam rather than a distinct school. According to most sources, approximately 85% of the world's Muslims are Sunni and approximately 15% are Shi'a, with a small minority who are members of other Islamic sects.

In modern times Islam has come under criticism from idealogues such as Robert Spencer and Ibn Warraq, who criticize Islamic law and question the morality of the Qur'an; for example, they say that its contents justify mistreatment of women and encourage antisemitic remarks by Muslim theologians; such claims are disputed by Muslim scholars. Montgomery Watt, Norman Daniel, and Edward Said dismiss many of the criticisms as the product of old myths and medieval European polemics. The rise of Islamophobia, according to Carl Ernst, had contributed to the negative views about Islam and Muslims in the West.

How one might harmonize Christianity and Islam

Most faith groups require their adherents to follow a specific group of beliefs. Comparing beliefs between two faith groups within the same religion or between two religions will often produce conflicts. However, it is possible for some to harmonize liberal/progressive Christianity with the basic tenets of Islam. It remains impossible to harmonize Islam with Christian fundamentalist and other evangelical denominations.

For example, most conservative and mainline Christian denominations expect their followers to believe in certain cardinal beliefs, such as:

- The Trinity - the belief that God is a unity consisting of three persons;

-

- The deity of Jesus;
- Jesus' bodily resurrection;
- The atonement as a result of the life, and particularly the death, of Jesus;
- The virgin birth; and
- The anticipated second coming of Jesus.

Most conservative Christian faith groups also include:

- Personal salvation by grace;
- The inerrancy of the Bible; and
- God's inspiration of the Bible's authors.

However, many liberal Christians and Progressive Christians believe that the Bible contains God's Word but is not God's word in its entirety. They may point to passages in the Hebrew Scriptures (Old Testament) that condoned and regulated human slavery, forced rape victims to marry their rapist, forced widows to marry their brother in law that described God ordering genocide, etc. They believe that God did not inspire the Bible's authors in the sense that he prevented them from including any errors in their writing. Rather, the authors wrote of their concepts of God, humanity, and the rest of the universe from within the limitations provided by their own culture and minimal scientific knowledge.

Many liberal and progressive Christians reject the concept of the Trinity and the deity of Christ, and believe as the original Christians did. During the early fourth decade CE, before the arrival of Paul, Jewish Christians in Jerusalem were the only known Christian movement. Their group was composed of reform Jews, and was founded by the followers of Jesus. They were led by James the brother of Jesus, and by Peter. They regarded Jesus as a great prophet, but as a human and not as a deity. They believed that God was single and indivisible. They engaged in animal sacrifices in the Temple, observed the Jewish holy days, followed kosher dietary laws and circumcised their male infants. By adopting the beliefs of these earliest Christians,

rather than modern-day believers, it is much easier to harmonize Islam and Christianity.

Two of the main beliefs of Islam:
That God is single and indivisible; and
That Jesus was a fully human, not divine, prophet;
are shared both by Muslims and by these original Christians. Potentially major stumbling blocks while harmonizing the two faiths involve the crucifixion, death and resurrection of Jesus, as well as criteria for individual.

Salvation: Christians, throughout history, have believed that the Roman Army crucified Jesus; that he died, was resurrected, and ascended to heaven. Most believe in the atonement -- that Jesus death gave some or all humans a path to salvation. Muslims believe, and the Qur'an teaches, that another person was crucified in Jesus' place. They believe that God would never have allowed his greatest prophet up to that time to be executed. They do not believe that Jesus was resurrected. They do believe that Jesus ascended bodily to Heaven, but at a later time than Christians believe. Many liberal and progressive Christians either reject or reinterpret the resurrection, ascension, salvation and atonement. On the positive side, most Christians and all or essentially all Muslims believe in Jesus' virgin birth and anticipate his second coming.

Hinduism

Hinduism is a religious tradition that originated in the Indian subcontinent. Hinduism is often referred to as *Sanātana Dharma* by its practitioners, a *Sanskrit* phrase meaning "the eternal law" [4] Hinduism is the world's oldest major religion that is still practiced. Its earliest origins can be traced to the ancient Vedic civilization. A conglomerate of diverse beliefs and traditions, Hinduism has no single founder. It is the world's third largest religion following Christianity and Islam, with approximately a billion adherents, of whom about 905 million live in

India and Nepal. Other countries with large Hindu populations include Bangladesh, Sri Lanka, Pakistan, Indonesia, Malaysia, Singapore, Mauritius, Fiji, Suriname, Guyana and Trinidad and Tobago.

Beliefs

Prominent themes in Hindu beliefs include *Dharma* (ethics/duties), *Samsāra* (The continuing cycle of birth, life, death and rebirth), *Karma* (action and subsequent reaction), *Moksha* (liberation from samsara), and the various *Yogas* (paths or practices).

Concept of God

Hinduism is a diverse system of thought with beliefs spanning monotheism, polytheism, panentheism, pantheism, monism and atheism. [5] It is sometimes referred to as henotheistic (devotion to a single God while accepting the existence of other gods), but any such term is an oversimplification of the complexities and variations of belief. Most Hindus believe that the spirit or soul—the true "self" of every person, called the *ātman*—is eternal. The goal of life according to the Advaita School is to realize that one's *ātman* is identical to Brahman, the supreme soul. The Upanishads state that whoever becomes fully aware of the *ātman* as the innermost core of one's own self, realizes their identity with Brahman and thereby reaches *Moksha* (liberation or freedom).

Karma and samsara

Karma translates literally as action, work or deed and can be described as the "moral law of cause and effect" [6] According to the Upanishads, an individual, known as the jiva-atma, develops *samskaras* (impressions) from actions, whether physical or mental. The "linga sharira", a body more subtle than the physical one, but less subtle than the soul, retains impressions, carrying them over into the next life, establishing a unique trajectory for the individual. Thus, the concept of a universal, neutral and never-failing karma intrinsically relates to reincarnation as well as one's personality, characteristics and family. Karma threads together the notions of free will and destiny.

This cycle of action, reaction, birth, death, and rebirth is a continuum called *samsara*. The notion of reincarnation and karma is a strong premise in Hindu thought. The *Bhagavad Gita* states that:
"As a person puts on new clothes and discards old and torn clothes, similarly an embodied soul enters new material bodies, leaving the old bodies.(B.G. 2:22)" [7] *Samsara* provides ephemeral pleasures, which lead people to desire rebirth to enjoy the pleasures of a perishable body. However, escaping the world of *samsara* through *moksha* (liberation) is believed to ensure lasting happiness and peace. It is thought that after several reincarnations, an *atman* eventually seeks unity with the cosmic spirit (*Brahman/Paramatman*).The ultimate goal of life, referred to as *moksha, nirvana* or *samadhi*, is understood in several different ways: as the realization of one's union with God; as realization of one's eternal relationship with God; realization of the unity of all existence; perfect unselfishness and knowledge of the Self; attainment of perfect mental peace; or as detachment from worldly desires. Such a realization liberates one from *samsara* and ends the cycle of rebirth. [8]

Hindu practices generally involve seeking awareness of God and sometimes also seeking blessings from *Devas*. Therefore, Hinduism has developed numerous practices meant to help one think of divinity in the midst of everyday life. Hindus can engage in *pūjā* (worship or veneration), either at home or at a temple. At home, Hindus often create a shrine with icons dedicated to the individual's chosen form(s) of God. Temples are usually dedicated to a primary deity along with associated subordinate deities though some commemorate multiple deities. Visiting temples is not obligatory. In fact, many visit temples only during religious festivals. Hindus perform their worship through icons (*murtis*). The icon serves as a tangible link between the worshiper and God. The image is often considered a manifestation of God, since God is immanent.[9] The Padma Purana states that the *mūrti* is not to be thought of as mere stone or wood but as a manifest form of the Divinity. A few Hindu sects, such as the Ārya Samāj, do not believe in worshiping God through icons.

Monasticism

Some Hindus choose to live a monastic life (*Sannyāsa*) in pursuit of liberation or another form of spiritual perfection. Monastics (*sādhus*) commit themselves to a life of simplicity, celibacy, detachment from worldly pursuits, and the contemplation of God. Some monastics live in monasteries, while others wander from place to place, trusting in God alone to provide for their needs. It is considered a highly meritorious act for a householder to provide *sādhus* with food or other necessaries. *Sādhus* strive to treat all with respect and compassion, whether a person may be poor or rich, good or wicked, and to be indifferent to praise, blame, pleasure, and pain. [10]

Varnas and the caste system

Hindu society has traditionally been categorized into four classes, called *Varnas:*

1. The *Brahmins*: teachers and priests;
2. The *Kshatriyas*: warriors, nobles, and kings;
3. The *Vaishyas*: farmers, merchants, and businessmen; and
4. The *Shudras*: servants and labourers.

There is controversy as to whether the caste system is an integral part of Hinduism sanctioned by the scriptures or an outdated social custom. Although the scriptures, since the Rigveda contain passages that clearly sanction the *Varna* system, they contain indications that the caste system is not an essential part of the religion. Both sides in the debate can find scriptural support for their views.

Ahimsa and vegetarianism

Hindus advocate the practice of ahi□sā (non-violence) and respect for all life because divinity is believed to permeate all beings, including plants and non-human animals. Estimates of the number of lacto vegetarians in India (includes inhabitants of all religions) vary between 20% and 42 %. Hindu society honors the cow as a symbol of unselfish giving. Cow-slaughter is legally banned in almost all states of India.[11]

Concepts of conversion, evangelization, and proselyzation are absent from Hindu literature and in practice have never played more than an insignificant role. This can generally be attributed to the fact that Hinduism considers all sincerely followed paths to god as equal. Hindu view of religious freedom is not based on the freedom to proselytize, but the right to retain one's religion and not be subject to proselyzation. Hindu leaders are advocating for changing the existing formulation of the freedom of religion clause in the Universal Declaration of Human Rights since it favors religions which proselytize.

Buddhism

Quotations

"Buddhism has the characteristics of what would be expected in a cosmic religion for the future: it transcends a personal God, avoids dogmas and theology; it covers both the natural & spiritual, and it is based on a religious sense aspiring from the experience of all things, natural and spiritual, as a meaningful unity"

-Albert Einstein

"The greatest achievement is selflessness.
The greatest worth is self-mastery.
The greatest quality is seeking to serve others.
The greatest precept is continual awareness.

The greatest medicine is the emptiness of everything.
The greatest action is not conforming with the worlds ways.
The greatest magic is transmuting the passions.

The greatest generosity is non-attachment.
The greatest goodness is a peaceful mind.
The greatest patience is humility.
The greatest effort is not concerned with results.
The greatest meditation is a mind that lets go.
The greatest wisdom is seeing through appearances."

-Atisha.

63

"If you live the sacred and despise the ordinary, you are still bobbing in the ocean of delusion."

-Lin-Chi.

"Aware of the suffering caused by the destruction of life, I vow to cultivate compassion and learn ways to protect lives of people, animals, plants, and minerals. I am determined not to kill, not to let others kill, and not to condone any killing in the world, in my thinking, and in my way of life."

-Ven. Thich Nhat Hanh.

Is Buddhism a religion?

Whether Buddhism is or is not a religion depends upon how you define "religion."
Government census offices and public opinion pollsters generally recognize Buddhism as a religion. Books that describe the religions of the world generally cover Buddhism along with Christianity, Islam, Hinduism, etc. Even the Boy Scouts of America, who expel Atheists, Agnostics and homosexuals, accept Buddhists as members. Like all major religions, Buddhism contains an explanation of the origin of existence, a morality, and a specific set of rituals and behaviors. ... Buddhism presents a transformational goal, a desire to improve one's situation, and a distinct moral code. However, some definitions of "religion" require a belief in the existence of one or more deities. That would disqualify most branches of Buddhism from being considered as religious groups.

With about 365 million followers - 6% of the world's population - Buddhism is the fourth largest religion in the world. It is exceeded in numbers only by Christianity, Islam and Hinduism. Buddhism was founded in Northern India by the first known Buddha, Siddhartha Gautama. In the sixth century BCE, he attained enlightenment and assumed the title Lord Buddha (one who has awakened). Buddhism later died out in India, but had become established in Sri Lanka. From there, it expanded across Asia, evolving into two or three main forms and traditions. Since the late 19th century Modern Buddhism has emerged as a truly international movement. It started as an attempt to produce a single form of Buddhism, without local accretions, that all Buddhists could embrace.

A Brief Overview of the Life of Buddha

Little is known about the Buddha's early life. No biography was written during his lifetime. Only isolated events from his life before he attained enlightenment were preserved. Some of the following are probably mythical in nature.

Traditional belief is that he was born a prince in Lumbinī, Nepal in the Terai lowlands near the foothills of the Himalayas. However, considerable archeological evidence now shows that he may have been born in Kalinga -- now Orissa in India. 7 He was a member of the Śākyas clan. His father, Suddhodana, was king of the clan. His mother was named Maya.There is no consensus on the date of his birth. Modern Buddhists of the Theravada tradition suggest he was born in 623 or 624 BCE. Until recently, many religious historians have preferred birth dates ranging from 567 to 487 BCE. Various modern scholars have suggested dates from 420 to 502 BCE. In short, nobody really knows.

In common with many other great religious leaders, many miraculous stories were associated with his birth. He emerged from his mother's side without causing her any pain. The earth shook as he was born. As a newborn, he was miraculously showered with water. He stood up, took seven steps, announced that he would be the "chief of the world." He also stated that this would be his last reincarnation. He was given the name Siddhãrtha Gautama. Siddhãrtha means "one who has achieved his aim." Gautama was his clan name. He was sometimes referred to as Śākyamuni which means "the sage of the Śākyas."He may have been born into the second of the four Indian castes -- the aristocratic warrior caste called Kṣatriyas.

Śākyamuni was raised as a Hindu. His parents assumed that he would succeed his father later in his life. His parents were concerned about a prophecy that astrologers gave at the time of his birth. They predicted that he would become either a universal monarch or a monk who would be a great religious teacher. His parents raised him in a state of luxury in the hope that he would become attached to earthly things and to pleasure. This would make it less likely that he choose the religious life.

At the age of 16, he was married to his wife Yaśodharã. When he was 29, his wife had a son, Rãhula. Shortly after his son's birth, some sources say that he took four journeys by chariot. Other sources say he had four visions. During the first trip/vision he was deeply disturbed by seeing an elderly, helpless, frail man. On the second, he saw an emaciated and depressed man suffering from an advanced disease. On the third, he spotted a grieving family carrying the corpse of one of their own to a cremation site. He reflected deeply upon the suffering brought about by old age, illness and death. On his fourth trip/vision, he saw a religious mendicant -- a śramaṇa -- who led a reclusive life of meditation, and was calm and serene. The four encounters motivated him to follow the path of the mendicant and find a spiritual solution to the problems brought about by human suffering. He left his wife, child, luxurious lifestyle, and future role as a leader of his people in order to seek truth. It was an accepted practice at the time for some men to leave their family and lead the life of an ascetic.

He first tried meditation, which he learned from two teachers. He felt that these were valuable skills. However, meditation could not be extended forever; He eventually had to return to normal waking consciousness and face the unsolved problems relating to birth, sickness, old age and death. He then joined a group of similarly-minded students of Brahmanism in a forest where he practiced breath control and fasted intensely for six years. He is said to have brought himself to the verge of death by only eating a few grains of rice each day. Some sources say that he consumed only a spoonful of bean soup per day. This technique produced a series of physical discomforts. Ultimately, he rejected this path as well. He realized that neither the extremes of the mortification of the flesh or of hedonism would lead to enlightenment. He determined that a better path to achieve the state of Nirvana -- a state of liberation and freedom from suffering - was to pursue "Middle Way." This way was largely defined by moderation and meditation.

One night In 535 BCE, at the age of 35, he was seated underneath a large tree -- later known as the Bodhi tree (species Pipal or ficus religiosus). He began to experience some major spiritual breakthroughs: During the first watch of the night, he developed the ability to recall the events of his previous reincarnations in detail. During the second watch, he was able to see how the good and bad deeds that many living entities performed during their lifetimes led to the nature of their subsequent reincarnation into their next life. During the third watch, he learned that he had progressed beyond "spiritual defilements," craving, desire, hatred, hunger, thirst, exhaustion, fear, doubt, and delusions. He had attained nirvana. He would never again be reincarnated into a future life. He had attained enlightenment! "He became a savior, deliverer, and redeemer."[12]The events under the Bodhi tree are often described in mythological terms in Buddhist literature and art. His experiences are portrayed as a battle with Mãra, the Buddhist equivalent of the Judeo-Christian-Islamic Satan.

After his enlightenment he assumed the title Lord Buddha (one who has awakened; the one who has attained enlightenment by himself). For seven days, he puzzled over his future: whether to withdraw from the world and live a life of seclusion, or whether to reenter the world and teach his Middle Way. He decided on the latter course: to proclaim his Dharma (teachings) to other humans so that they could also attain enlightenment. He located five of his fellow seekers with whom he had earlier fasted, and rejoined them near Benares. They quickly became aware of the changes brought about by his enlightenment. It was to them that he preached his first sermon. It contained the essential teachings of Buddhism. All five accepted his teachings and were ordained as monks. After the Buddha's second sermon, all five achieved enlightenment. They are referred to as Arhants (saints).

The Buddha's later life

He wandered around Northeast India for decades, teaching all who would listen. He had tens of thousands of disciples and accumulated a large public following. He later established an order of monks and a corresponding order of nuns. His wife Yaśodharā became the first nun.His health began to fail when he was in this late 70s. After forty-five years of teaching, he died in a small town named Kuśinagara, at the age of 80, apparently of natural causes. His final words were: "Decay is inherent in all things. Be sure to strive with clarity of mind" for Nirvana. The traditional date of his death used by Theravadin Buddhists is 544 or 543 BCE. However, dates have been suggested from 544 to 380 BCE. He did not choose a successor. He felt that the Dharma -- his teachings -- plus the Vinaya -- his code of rules for the monks and nuns -- would be a sufficient guide. Two and a half centuries later, a council of Buddhist monks collected his teachings and the oral traditions of the faith into written form, called the Tripitaka. This included a very large collection of commentaries and traditions; most are called Sutras (discourses).

Core beliefs of Buddhism:

Buddhism, like most of the great religions of the world, is divided into a number of different traditions. However, most traditions share a common set of fundamental beliefs. One of the fundamental beliefs of Buddhism is often referred to as reincarnation -- the concept that people are reborn after dying. In fact, most individuals go through many cycles of birth, living, death and rebirth. A practicing Buddhist differentiates between the concepts of rebirth and reincarnation. In reincarnation, the individual may recur repeatedly. In rebirth, in a person does not necessarily return to Earth as the same entity ever again. He compares it to a leaf growing on a tree. When the withering leaf falls off, a new leaf will eventually replace it. It is similar to the old leaf, but it is not identical to the original leaf. After many such cycles, if a person releases their attachment to desire and the self, they can attain Nirvana. This is a state of liberation and freedom from suffering.

The Three Trainings and Practices

Sila: Virtue, good conduct, morality. This is based on two fundamental principles: The principle of equality: that all living entities are equal.

The principle of reciprocity: This is the "Golden Rule" in Christianity -- to do onto others as you would wish them do onto you. It is found in all major religions.

Samadhi: Concentration, meditation, mental development. Developing one's mind is the path to wisdom which in turn leads to personal freedom. Mental development also strengthens and controls our mind; this helps us maintain good conduct.

Prajna: Discernment, insight, wisdom, enlightenment. This is the real heart of Buddhism. Wisdom will emerge if your mind is pure and calm. The first two paths listed in the Eightfold Path, described below, refer to discernment; the last three belong to concentration; the middle three are related to virtue.

The Four Noble Truths

The Buddha's Four Noble Truths explore human suffering. They may be described (somewhat simplistically) as:
Dukkha: Suffering exists: (Suffering is real and almost universal. Suffering has many causes: loss, sickness, pain, failure, the impermanence of pleasure.)
Samudaya: There is a cause for suffering. (It is the desire to have and control things. It can take many forms: craving of sensual pleasures; the desire for fame; the desire to avoid unpleasant sensations, like fear, anger or jealousy.)
Nirodha: There is an end to suffering. (Suffering ceases with the final liberation of *Nirvana* (a.k.a. *Nibbana*). The mind experiences complete freedom, liberation and non-attachment. It lets go of any desire or craving.
Magga: In order to end suffering, you must follow the Eightfold Path.

The Five Precepts

These are rules to live by. They are somewhat analogous to the second half of the Ten Commandments in Judaism and Christianity -- that part of the Decalogue which describes behaviors to avoid. However, they are recommendations, not commandments. Believers are expected to use their own intelligence in deciding exactly how to apply these rules.

Do not kill. This is sometimes translated as "not harming" or an absence of violence.

Do not steal. This is generally interpreted as including the avoidance of fraud and economic exploitation.

Do not lie. This is sometimes interpreted as including name calling, gossip, etc.

Do not misuse sex. For monks and nuns, this means any departure from complete celibacy. For the laity, adultery is forbidden, along with any sexual harassment or exploitation, including that within marriage. The Buddha did not discuss consensual premarital sex within a committed relationship; Buddhist traditions differ on this.

Do not consume alcohol or other drugs. The main concern here is that intoxicants cloud the mind. Some have included as a drug other methods of divorcing ourselves from reality -- e.g. movies, television, the Internet.[13]

The Eightfold Path

The Buddha's Eightfold Path [14] consists of:
 Discernment, wisdom; Right Understanding of the Four Noble Truths; Right thinking; following the right path in life; Virtue, morality; Right speech: no lying, criticism, condemning, gossip, harsh language; Right conduct by following the Five Precepts; Right livelihood; support yourself without harming others; Concentration, meditation; Right Effort: promote good thoughts; conquer evil thoughts; Right Mindfulness: Become aware of your body, mind and feelings; Right Concentration: Meditate to achieve a higher state of consciousness

Walter Taminang

Comparison of Buddhism with Christianity

Beliefs not shared

Buddhists do not share most of the core beliefs of historical Christianity and many of the less critical beliefs accepted by some Christians. Buddhism does not teach:

- An original golden era in the Garden of Eden, and a subsequent fall of humanity.
- Original sin shared by all present-day humans, derived from Adam and Eve.
- A world-wide flood in the time of Noah, causing the greatest human genocide in history.
- The need for a sinless personal savior whose execution enabled individual salvation through atonement.
- A god-man savior who was born of a virgin, executed, resurrected and ascended to heaven.
- Salvation achieved through good works (a traditional liberal Christian belief) or through specific beliefs (as in conservative Protestant faith groups) and/or sacraments (as in the Roman Catholic Church).
- Eternal life spent in either a heaven or hell after death.
- Return of a savior to earth at some time in the future.
- An end of the world as we know it in the near future.

Some shared beliefs

Buddhism and Christianity share some features:

Ethic of Reciprocity: Buddhism, Christianity and all of the other major world religions share a basic rule of behavior which governs how they are to treat others. Two quotations from Buddhist texts which reflect this Ethic are: "...a state that is not pleasing or delightful to me, how could I inflict that upon another?" Samyutta NIkaya v. 353. Hurt not others in ways that you yourself would find hurtful." Udana-Varga 5:18. This compares closely to Christianity's Golden Rule, which is seen in: "Therefore all things whatsoever ye would that men hould do to you, do ye even so to them." Matthew 7:12.

Life after death: Almost all religions teach that a person's personality continues after death. In fact, many religious historians believe that this belief was the prime reason that motivated people to originally create religions. Christianity and Buddhism are no exception. However, they conceive of life after death in very different forms: Buddhism teaches that humans are trapped in a repetitive cycle of birth, life, death and rebirth. One's goal is to escape from this cycle and reach Nirvana. Once this is attained, the mind experiences complete freedom, liberation and non-attachment. Suffering ends because desire and craving -- the causes of suffering -- are no more. Christianity has historically taught that everyone has only a single life on earth. After death, an eternal life awaits everyone: either in Heaven or Hell. There is no suffering in Heaven; only joy. Torture is eternal without any hope of cessation for the inhabitants of Hell.

Themes of morality, justice, love: These themes are found through both the Buddha's teaching and the Hebrew and Christian Bible.

Judaism

Judaism is the religion of the Jewish people, based on principles and ethics embodied in the Hebrew Bible (Tanakh) and the Talmud. According to Jewish tradition, the history of Judaism begins with the Covenant between God and Abraham (ca. 2000 BCE), the patriarch and progenitor of the Jewish people. Judaism is among the oldest religious traditions still in practice today. Jewish history and doctrines have influenced other religions such as Christianity, Islam and the Bahá'í Faith.

While Judaism has seldom, if ever, been monolithic in practice, it has always been monotheistic in theology. It differs from many religions in that central authority is not vested in a person or group, but in sacred texts and traditions. Throughout the ages, Judaism has clung to a number of religious principles, the most important of which is the belief in a single, omniscient, omnipotent, benevolent, transcendent God, who created the universe and continues to govern it. According to traditional Jewish belief, the God who created the world established a covenant with the Israelites, and revealed his laws and commandments to Moses on Mount Sinai in the form of the Torah, and the Jewish people are the descendants of the Israelites. The traditional practice of Judaism revolves around study and the observance of God's laws and commandments as written in the Torah and expounded in the Talmud.

Early History of Judaism

According to the Hebrew Scriptures:
Circa 2000 BCE, the G-d * of the ancient Israelites established a divine covenant with Abraham, making him the patriarch of many nations. The book of Genesis describes the events surrounding the lives of the three patriarchs: Abraham, Isaac, and Jacob.

(Joseph, who is recognized as a fourth patriarch by Christians is not considered one by Jews). Moses was the next major leader of the ancient Israelites. He led his people out of captivity in Egypt, and received the Mosaic Law from G-d. After decades of wandering through wilderness, Joshua led the tribes into the Promised Land, driving out the Canaanites through a series of military battles. The original tribal organization was converted into a kingdom by Samuel; its first king was Saul. The second king, David, established Jerusalem as the religious and political center. The third king, Solomon built the first temple there. Division into the Northern kingdom of Israel and the Southern kingdom of Judah occurred shortly after the death of Solomon in 922 BCE. Israel fell to Assyria in 722 BCE; Judah fell to the Babylonians in 587 BCE. The temple was destroyed.

Some Jews returned from captivity under the Babylonians and started to restore the temple in 536 BCE. (Orthodox Jews date the Babylonian exile from 422 to 352 BCE). Alexander the Great invaded the area in 332 BCE. From circa 300 to 63 BCE, Greek became the language

---

*The term "G-d" is used here to respect the Jewish prohibition against spelling the name or title of the deity in full.

of commerce, and Greek culture had a major influence on Judaism. In 63 BCE, the Roman Empire took control of Judea and Israel.

Jewish developments during the 1st century CE

About 24 religious sects had formed by the 1st century CE of which the largest were the Basusim, Essenes, Pharisees, Sadducees and Zealots. Many anticipated the arrival of the Messiah, a religious-political-military leader who was expected to drive out the Roman invaders and restore independence.

Christianity was established initially as a Jewish sect, centered in Jerusalem. The group followed the teachings of Yeshua of Nazareth, who is now commonly referred to as Jesus Christ. The group was led by James, one of Jesus' four brothers. They are generally referred to as Jewish Christians. Paul broke with this tradition, created an alternative belief system of Pauline Christianity and spread the religion to the Gentiles (non-Jews). A third religion, Gnosticism, emerged in a number of forms, such as Christian and Jewish Gnosticism. Many mini-revolts led to the destruction of Jerusalem and its temple in 70 CE. The Jewish Christians were wiped out or scattered at this time. The movement started by Paul flourished and quickly evolved into the religion of Christianity. Jews were scattered throughout the known world. Their religion was no longer centered in Jerusalem; Jews were prohibited from setting foot there. Judaism became decentralized and stopped seeking converts. The local synagogue became the new center of Jewish life. Animal sacrifice was abandoned. Authority shifted from the centralized priesthood to local scholars and teachers, giving rise to Rabbinic Judaism.

The period from the destruction of the temple onward give rise to heavy persecution by Christians throughout Europe and Russia. Many groundless stories were spread, accusing Jews of ritual murder, the desecration of the Catholic host and continuing responsibility for the execution of Jesus. Unsubstantiated rumors continue to be circulated today. In the 1930s and 1940s, Adolph Hitler and the German Nazi party drew on centuries of Christian-based anti-Semitism, and upon their own psychotic beliefs in racial purity. They organized the Holocaust, the attempted extermination of all Jews in Europe. About 6 million were killed in one of the world's greatest examples of religious and racial intolerance.

The Zionist movement was a response within all Jewish traditions to centuries of Christian persecution. Their initial goal was create a Jewish homeland in Palestine. The state of Israel was formed on 1948-MAY-18. There are currently about 18 million Jews throughout the world. They are mainly concentrated in North America (about 7 million) and Israel (about 4.5 million).

Jewish Texts

The *Tanakh* corresponds to the Jewish Scriptures, (often referred to as the Old Testament by Christians). It is composed of three groups of books: the *Torah* (aka Pentateuch): Genesis, Exodus, Leviticus, Numbers and Deuteronomy. the Nevi'im: Joshua, Judges, Samuel (2), Kings (2), Isaiah, Jeremiah, Ezekiel, Hosea, Joel, Amos, Obadiah, Jonah, Micah, Nahum, Habakkuk, Zephaniah, Haggai, Zachariah, and MalachiIsaiah.

 The *Ketuvim*, the "Writings" including Psalms, Proverbs, Job, Song of Songs, Ecclesiastes, Ruth, Esther, Lamentations, Daniel, Ezra, Nehemiah, Chronicles.
The Talmud contains stories, laws, medical knowledge, debates about moral choices, etc. It is composed of material which comes mainly from two sources:

The *Mishnah's*, "orders" containing hundreds of chapters, including series of laws from the Hebrew Scriptures, was compiled about 200 CE.

 The *Gemara* (one Babylonian and one Palestinian) is encyclopedic in scope. It includes comments from hundreds of Rabbis from 200 - 500 CE, explaining the *Mishnah* with additional historical, religious, legal, sociological, etc. material. It often records many different opinions on a topic without giving a definitive answer.

Basic Jewish Beliefs:

There is a story in wide circulation about a question asked of Rabbi

Hillel -- a notable rabbi from the 1st century BCE. A non-Jew asked the rabbi to teach him everything about the Torah while standing on one foot. Rabbi Hillel responded: "What is hateful to you, don't do unto your neighbor. The rest is commentary. Now, go and study." Rabbi Moshe ben Maimon, (a.k.a. Maimonides) is generally accepted as one of the most important Jewish scholars from medieval times. He wrote a list of thirteen principles of faith. This list has been generally accepted by Jews for centuries as a brief summary of the Jewish faith. However, the liberal wings of Judaism dispute some of the 13 today.

- G-d exists.
- G-d is one and unique.
- G-d is incorporeal.
- G-d is eternal.

Prayer is to be directed to G-d alone and to no other.
The words of the prophets are true.

Moses was the greatest of the prophets, and his prophecies are true.
The Written Torah (first 5 books of the Bible) and Oral Torah (teachings now contained in the Talmud and other writings) were given to Moses.
There will be no other Torah.
G-d knows the thoughts and deeds of men.
G-d will reward the good and punish the wicked.
The Messiah will come.
The dead will be resurrected. [14]

Additional Jewish beliefs

Some additional beliefs found commonly among Jews are:
Some Jews view Jesus as a great moral teacher. Others see him as a false prophet or as an idol of Christianity. Some sects of Judaism will not even say his name due to the prohibition against saying an idol's name. The Jews are often referred to as G-d's chosen people. This does not mean that they are in any way to be considered superior to other groups. Biblical verses such as Exodus 19:5 simply imply that G-d has selected Israel to receive and study the Torah, to worship G-d only, to rest on the weekly Sabbath, and to celebrate the festivals. Jews

were not chosen to be better than others; they were simply selected to receive more difficult responsibilities and more onerous punishment if they fail. The 613 commandments found in Leviticus and other books regulate all aspects of Jewish life.

The Ten Commandments, as delineated in Exodus 20:1-17 and Deuteronomy 5:6-21, form a brief synopsis of the Law. The Messiah (the anointed one of G-d) will arrive in the future and gather Jews once more into the land of Israel. There will be a general resurrection of the dead at that time. The Jerusalem Temple, destroyed in 70 CE, will be rebuilt. A fetus gains full personhood when it is half-emerged from its mother's body. Boys reach the status of Bar Mitzvah on their 13th birthday; girls reach Bat Mitzvah on their 12th birthday. This means that they are recognized as adults and are personally responsible to follow the Jewish commandments and laws. Males are allowed to lead a religious service; they are counted in a "minyan" (a quota of men necessary to perform certain parts of religious services). Following their Bar Mitzvah or Bat Mitzvah they can sign contracts; they can testify in religious courts; theoretically, they can marry, although the Talmud recommends 18 to 24 as the proper age for marriage.
The more liberal movements within Judaism differ from some of the above beliefs concerning the source of the Torah, the concept of direct reward and punishment according to one's behavior, etc.

Jewish Practices

They include: Observation of the weekly Sabbath as a day of rest, starting at sundown on Friday evening; strict discipline, according to the Law, which governs all areas of life; regular attendance by Jewish males at Synagogue; celebration of the annual festivals including: **Passover**, or *Pesach* is held each Spring to recall the Jews' deliverance out of slavery in Egypt circa 1300 BCE. A ritual Seder meal is eaten in each observant Jewish home at this time. Six different foods are placed on the seder plate in the order in which they area eaten: *Karpas* (vegetables dipped in salt water) recalls the bitter tears shed during slavery, *Maror* (bitter herbs) to symbolize the bitterness of slavery

Chazeret (bitter vegetables) also to symbolize the bitterness of slavery

Choroset (apple, nuts & spices with wine) represents the mortar used by Hebrew slaves. Also placed on the seder plate, but uneaten during the Seder meal: *Zeroa* (lamb shankbone) to recall the Passover sacrifice in the ancient temple; *Beitzah* (roasted egg) symbolizes mourning, sacrifice, spring, and renewal. Not placed on the Seder plate, but often eaten, is a boiled egg. After women were first allowed to become *Rabbim*, some Jews commented: "A woman belongs as a Rabbi like an orange belongs on a seder plate." As such, many Reform Jews now include an orange with their Seder Plate to commemorate female Rabbim.

Rosh Hashanah is the Jewish New Year, and is the anniversary of the completion of creation, about 5760 years ago. It is held in the fall. The 10 days from Rosh Hashanah to *Yom Kippur*, the Day of Atonement, are days of penitence. *Yom Kippur* is a day of fasting until sundown.

Sukkoth or the Feast of Booths, is an 8 day harvest festival; a time of thanksgiving.

Hanukkah or the Feast of Lights, is an 8 day feast of dedication. It recalls the war fought by the Maccabees in the cause of religious freedom. It also commemorates a miracle in the Temple, when one-day's worth of oil lasted eight days. It is typically observed in December. Originally a minor Jewish holy day, it has become more important in recent years.

Purim, the Feast of Lots recalls the defeat by Queen Esther of the plan to slaughter all of the Persian Jews, circa 400 BCE.

Shavout, the Feast of Weeks recalls G-d's revelation of the Torah to the Jewish people. It is held in late May or early June.

The local synagogue is governed by the congregation and is normally led by a rabbi who has been chosen by the congregation. Any adult male with sufficient knowledge can lead religious services. In reform and some conservative congregations, a woman can also preside. This is often done in those Jewish communities who lack a rabbi.

Judaism and Christianity compared

Although Christians base much of their faith on the same Hebrew Scriptures as Jews, there are major differences in belief:

- Jews are strict monotheists: they view G-d as a single, indivisible entity. Most Christians view God as a Trinity: a single entity with three personalities -- the Father, Son and Holy Spirit.
- Jews generally consider actions and behavior to be of primary importance; beliefs come out of actions. This conflicts with conservative Christians for whom belief is of primary importance and actions tend to be derivative from beliefs.
- Jewish belief does not accept the Christian concept of original sin (the belief that all people have inherited Adam and Eve's sin when they disobeyed G-d's instructions in the Garden of Eden).
- Judaism affirms the inherent goodness of the world and its people as creations of G-d.
- Jewish believers are able to sanctify their lives and draw closer to G-d by performing fulfilling *mitzvot* (divine commandments).
- Jews do not recognize the need for a savior as an intermediary with G-d.

Pluralist Model of Religion

Religious Pluralism is the belief that no single religion should be privileged and that people of all faith communities or none should be respected and allowed to live by the principles of their tradition without interference as long as those principles do not call followers to harm others. In the United States (and many other Western nations) the implementation of religious pluralism is a guiding principle protected by law and is closely related to the separation of church and state. But for ordinary people hoping to live peacefully in a community, at least as important as the officially guaranteed liberty of religion and conscience, is the attitude of their neighbors who identify with a different religion or denomination. In the latter sense, especially, religious pluralism is diametrically opposed to fundamentalism which assumes that the teachings of a particular religious tradition interpreted a certain, unchanging way, represent an absolute truth and that

consequently all other interpretations, religions, and ideologies are in
error and in need of being corrected.
Religious pluralism endorses the following key Principles:

1. Inter-religious dialogue and engagement should be the way
   for religions to relate to one another. A paramount need is
   for religions to heal antagonisms among themselves.
2. The dialogue should engage the pressing problems of the
   world today, including war, violence, poverty,
   environmental devastation, gender injustice, and violation of
   human rights.
3. Absolute truth claims can easily be exploited to incite
   religious hatred and violence.
4. The religions of the world affirm ultimate reality/truth which
   is conceptualized in different ways.
5. While ultimate reality/truth is beyond the scope of complete
   human understanding, it has found expression in diverse
   ways in the world's religions.
6. The great world religions with their diverse teachings and
   practices constitute authentic paths to the supreme good.
7. The world's religions share many essential values, such as
   love, compassion, equality, honesty, and the ideal of treating
   others as one wishes to be treated oneself.
8. All persons have freedom of conscience and the right to
   choose their own faith.
9. While mutual witnessing promotes mutual respect,
   proselytizing devalues the faith of the other.
   (http://www.metareligion.org/model.htm)

This set of key principles simply means that the One we call God, the
Really Real, can be approached in an infinite number of different
ways, all of which are legitimate, as long as they don't call us to break
the only unconditional Prime Directive: always to act in the most
loving, caring, humane manner possible under given circumstances.
Religious Pluralism does not call us to abandon our religious
traditions. It calls us to expand and deepen our definition of
religiousness and spirituality to include the simple, self evident
premise that the very fact that I expect others to respect my right to

view the Really Real through my unique set of lenses means that I am morally obligated to grant them the same privilege.

In his classic book, *Survival of the Wisest*, Salk[15] argued that sustained improvements in quality of life require embracing what he called "the characteristics of an 'and' rather than an 'or', philosophy-an 'additive' philosophy rather than an 'alternative' one". He characterized the "enemy" to effective problem solving not as those who hold alternative views or who come from different perspectives or disciplines "but rather as those who are pathologically divisive or destructive of the unification and coalescence of healthy, contributing, constructive elements of greater complexity necessary to solve problems.

Vladimir Tomek[16] in his brilliant essay decrying religious intolerance posits as follows:

- The spiritual basis for religious tolerance is the recognition of the common source of all the world's great faiths.
- Among the basic human rights, the right to follow one's conscience in matters of religion and belief is undoubtedly one of the most cherished.
- Our picture of the ultimate reality is influenced by an unavoidable selection effect – that of our existence. Our human mind always sees everything from a limited and hence incomplete perspective: It is most difficult to discuss any religious issue without taking sides. In this respect, consider the damage done in religious schools, where children in their earliest years are encouraged to view life through the prism of a particular religious doctrine and cultural prejudices, thus acquiring a biased view for life.

- We are better informed that our parents and grandparents were. We must use this extra knowledge. If we want to resolve some of the difficulties religions face, our deliberations will have to be brought down from the level of theological abstractions to the level of specific problems that are urgent and typical. Some help may come from philosophy, but the expectations do not seem to be particularly bright – by its very nature, philosophy is rather inconclusive.

- Religions rarely publicize their opponents' true views, perhaps because they might be found persuasive. It is considered far better to put a spin on things oneself, to show how absurd the opposition's ideas are, how problematic, how dangerous. Do we really know what the early Christian heretics, such as Marcion, taught when most of what we know about him is derived from attacks on his ideas by orthodox writers'?

- Although universal religion is still just an utopia, a determined attempt should be made at the reconciliation of different systems of belief, which would leave room for intelligent disagreement.

In view of the present widespread religious intolerance and fundamentalism threatening our very existence, I personally think that what the world desperately needs is a honing of the skills of explication, of dialogue, of logic and rhetoric; a honing of the skills of compassion, which just like intellectual abilities, need practice to be perfected. There is a global close-mindedness that imperils the species. Although this has always been with us, the dangers are now graver because weapons of mass destruction masterminded by modern scientific advances and encouraged by fundamentalist regimes, are becoming more and more commonplace. The fact is, we face a difficult and uncertain future if this unfortunate trend should persist.

5

Limitations of Science

"...science is a very successful way of knowing, but not the only way...A scientific view of the world is hopelessly incomplete. Science seeks material explanations for material processes, but it has nothing definitive to say about realities beyond its scope. Once science has had its say, there remain questions of value, purpose, and meaning that are forever beyond science's domain, but belong in the realm of philosophical reflection and religious experience"

-Francisco J. Ayala, Professor of biological sciences and of philosophy at the University of California, Irvine)

What is science? To know its limitations, one must know its extent. Science is concerned with relating effects to causes; it walks backwards from what it 'did'; and if it sometimes sees something of the future reflected in the past, it is more concerned with reflection than reality. Science is common sense in close focus. Common sense, with my unaided eyes, may tell me that a table is smooth; commonsense, with a microscope, may tell me that the same table is rough; and common sense with an electron microscope, may tell me that this same table again is a conglomeration of spatial relationships between electrical charges. Each opinion is correct in context; each opinion contradicts the other two; each opinion is common sense. Opinion depends upon available data, and it is foolish to suggest that common sense runs counter to scientific discovery. But each of these three versions of that table 'works'; its smoothness responds to the housewife's polish; its roughness rewards the table tennis player's spin; and its spatial texture accept the technician's processes. Although truth may not be assailed by belief, it may, perhaps, prove adaptable to faith. In another sense than the imposition of patterns in ordering of knowledge, we may be found to impose designs upon belief and to prove them workable.

The doctor, with his drugs and his hormones, his secretions and his detailed knowledge of anatomy and what repairs it, often attains considerable and often spectacular success in the treatment of disease; but so, too, does the specialist in acupuncture, a system based entirely on original metaphysical concepts. Either it seems, is truth. Even more striking in many ways is the placebo effect, whereby the 'controls' dosed with an imaginary drug display the same progressive responses as those receiving the drug designed to produce them.

Science deals with statistics; it can measure the decay of radium, but it cannot tell which particular atoms in any mass of the metal will be the next to change. It knows how much, but not which. It reduces color to wavelengths. Its hard cold instruments disconnect fact from reality, and we cannot overlook that both are altered by the operation-the facts absolutely and the reality relatively. To observe is to alter. The fact we establish by scientific means is different from the fact if we had not established it. Matter is in a way self-conscious; it reacts to the watcher in his watching; and it seems possible that the eternal verities are by their nature the truths that science cannot reveal. The use of measurements has enabled science to make enormous strides in the understanding of the material universe. The downside of this is that scientists have come to regard measurement as a scientific idol, leading to a widespread attitude of skepticism among many scientists about what cannot be measured. Things that cannot be directly measured are considered incapable of being known, and thus unimportant. This attitude to me constitutes a form of bigotry similar to religious bigotry and fundamentalism.

Matter is motion. But matter can be construed within certain forms; and even living matter changing continuously leaves its forms recognizable and their identities intact while it passes through them. A constitution remains though its membership alters, and it becomes apparent that the dichotomy between matter and life, perhaps between nature and spirit, is the difference between flux and form. Stillness is of the mind alone; and perhaps of the self alone is permanence.

The difference between man and what he is made of runs implicitly through all his professions; in his crafts he is outside the things he fashions; in his arts, he is within the expression of his thoughts; in both he is of himself aware, and the harder he struggles to impress intention in material, the more he realizes his separated consciousness: the artist knows this as he toils to spread less paint than picture on his canvas; the poet knows it as he tries with words for meanings; and the musician knows it as he struggles to discover the noise of truth.

If the things of the spirit are stillness and the things of the flesh are change, then it is obvious that the values of the spirit are qualitative, and quantitative those of the flesh. Changes are measurable; stillness appreciable. The analyst will find salt in tears, the poet sorrow; but the latter may be wrong to discern heartbeats in the pulsing salinities of seas: the conclusions of the scientist may be inadequate; but the analogies of the artist can be ludicrous. From this we might be led to suspect that truth is divisible, until we realize that the quantitative and the qualitative come together in brain and mind. They are joined, not parted. And we come then to the possible idea that life is what brings together the things that happen and the things that are, the measurable and the absolute, time as the arbiter and consequence of events and eternity as the container of it all.

In faith, belief precedes or exceeds knowledge; and the full religious life is a process of perpetual realization. In science, assumption goes before disproof; and the stark scientific life is a way of continual remission. Yet are the two so much different or does the change lie in the people who follow them? May it not merely be that the opposed viewpoints make the same seem different; that the scientist in retreat from his experiments sees their background in the inert past, while the devotee pursuing his belief is aware of his horizon rising to opening firmaments? And the disciple who believes a little more than he knows may be, in reality, very little removed from the skeptic who tries out as much as proof will stretch to.

Perhaps the fundamental issue between the scientist and the non-scientist is that the former regards as true only what is susceptible of experimental proof. He does not believe in what happens, but only in what can happen again. In a sense he is concerned with the sameness of events, whereas, the religious man is set on the unrepeatable variety of experience. Science is quite logical. Yet logic must follow on premises, and however far back science may push its axioms, however basic may become its origins, it can find no absolute beginnings. And the farther back or the more deeply basic they lie, the longer the chain of reasoning, then the more likely it is that some remote error, however slight, may have thrown the subsequent line of logic wide off its true course. The danger of close logic is that one deviation throws the total conclusion wrong, whereas the mystic experience of the religious and the intuitive sources of the artist can, by their nature, compensate for the incidence of error.

Two immediate effects follow from the dedicated neutrality of the scientist and the dispassionate means at his disposal. First, his freedom from opinion can lead to the lack of belief; and his methods of assessment can lead to absence of values. The emptying of opinion has carried a loss of option, and he increases his knowledge at the possible expense of understanding; and he runs the risk of applying his knowledge with the same disinterest as he gives in gathering it.

As we move up the scientific scale from the basic to life sciences and on to social sciences, we find the penalties of abstraction increase. The biologist has to examine items in which change and decay occur during the process of examination. The vivisectionist does not study the creature, but the wounded creature; not its organs but its excisions. The part of the creature he takes for study is no longer part of the creature; and if he removed an organ to examine the functioning of the creature without it, the effect is obscured by the side-effects. And while he may have taken 'short-cuts' to useful knowledge, it is doubtful whether in the process, he has not lost clues to vital understanding.

Consciousness almost certainly depends upon the reception of signals from many parts of the body and with these cut out, consciousness as we know it is unlikely to occur. Truth is, the mechanism and nature of consciousness is hardly understood at all and the nightmarish situation that, even remotely, could arise within a disembodied brain leaves little latitude for permissiveness in such experiments. And while not denying science the right to probe, it is worth remembering that the recognition of consciousness in other men and other animals is what distinguishes a humanitarian.

 As applied science is open to misunderstanding, so then, of pure science we can say that scientific disinterest can make for scientists' nihilism; that scientific method can destroy a sense of worth; and that as science is organized into its parts it is disorganized as a whole. We have numerous views and no vision, like maps without a globe, as each flat diagram departs from the sphere of its activities, so the smaller area covered by each projection the more accurate it is, yet the more numerous the errors and their totality greater. Scientific rectitude is preserved by limitation of its fields, and scientific integrity shattered in the process. If all the maps of an exhaustive atlas were fitted together they would not even approximate to the sweep of truth. The skin of the earth, however limited is boundless. Knowledge is fractionalized and the wholeness of creation forgotten. We have overlooked the gestalt in finding the part. We cannot see the truth for the facts. Truth and facts are different. Facts may be part of truth, but not the whole truth.

The fundamental assumption of science is that hypotheses can be checked; that theories can be put into practice; that experiments can be repeated. This basic assumption is open to question. It must be agreed that experiments may be similar; but it must also be asserted that they cannot be identical. No two castings from the same mould are ever wholly alike. Allowance must be made for experimental variation and here again statistical methods come to the scientist's aid. He starts taking averages and plotting curves. He takes the average of repeated experiments and the refinements of better ones. His truth is the latest but never the last. Indeed, if a series of experiments show a close approximation to each other and to the hypothesized result except for one or two aberrant results well outside the norm of laboratory error, then the scientists, with St Paul, will take only 'those things that are good report'.

Of course, scientists know that nothing, not even by chance, is ever completely repeatable, because change, however minute, is persistent. The universe expands, materials radio-actively decay; the heavier elements congeal. And because no single atom is unaffected by all the other atoms in the universe, science has no finality; it moves, like man himself, between yesterday and tomorrow without beginning or end, upon a shifting ground. Hoyle, the astronomer, looking not only into distances before him but into his and our remotest past, has hazarded that the totality of change of the past 5 billion years of the earth's existence, may be such as to give us today natural laws themselves different from those which once applied.

The basic stuffs of science are matter and energy. These were once held separate; they are now found to be interchangeable. Each can be assessed in terms of the other, and nuclear physicists can measure and execute the change from one to the other; it is measured in standard units as well as, at Hiroshima in personal ones. But while we can exchange matter for energy and energy for matter, we still have no idea of the basic entity which is both of them. We can discern the phenomena, not the reality; what happens, not what is. And we have not the faintest explanation of the consciousness by which we are, even so narrowly, aware of these things. Nor, indeed can we be certain that matter and energy sum up the totality of existence. Apart from consciousness, which cannot be related to either however much it uses them; or beauty which, however much they display it, cannot be reduced to them; or experience, which is so much more than the phenomena that make it and indeed so much varied from the same phenomena; apart from these, there are gaps between the scientific disciplines and voids about them averse to instrumental treatment; and there are conceptions used in the process of science, which have no part in its results.

The theories of conservation of energy and matter (now necessarily combined) are widely, but not exhaustively applicable. For example, matter and anti-matter are considered mutually exclusive and symmetrically destructive. If equal quantities of both are brought together, they disappear in a flash of energy. But where does the energy come from? It is, apparently, extra to the matter and the anti-matter; as in M-M=E instead of O. Anyway, why should energy be evolved instead of anti-energy, whatever that may be? And what happens to Potential Energy if pushed too far? And how does the theory of conservation stand up to the facts of cosmology? Hoyle's 'steady state' theory, now, perhaps, tottering on its hypothetical legs, asserts the continuous creation of matter (one hydrogen atom per seven cubic miles of space). Ryle's "Big bang" stipulates a creative event in, or at, the beginning of time-an explosion of the locked energies of the "Great Atom" without an explanation of what locked them. The only plausible alternative, the theory of a pulsating universe, has so far been touched upon too lightly for its mechanisms to be guessed; possibly the momentum of expansion might be slowed down by the friction of inter-galactic matter if we could except that from the embryo universe; and the contraction when it comes might be gravitationally induced towards a new explosion of its gathered forces. Such a theory might be worked out consistently with conservation, but even then some heat would be dissipated by the drag of not-quite-empty- space (a heat sufficient to account for the total brake energy exerted), and a certain extra-cosmic entropy would have to be substituted for the infra-cosmic energies of the other two theories.

No explanation in wholly material terms can be given for those natural anomalies which alone make life possible; two examples will suffice. Water, unlike other substances, expands below 4 degrees centigrade and freezes lighter than the liquid to allow, instead of perma-frost, the 18-inch thin skin of fertile earth which is our only habitat. The light from the stars should be more than enough to give high noon at all hours of such intensity that life anywhere would be impossible; yet this light is softened by the alleged recession of the galaxies and reduced to an approximately desirable amount by the absorptive effects of interstellar dust, and finally trimmed to an accurate dosage by the flutter of our own atmosphere. There is no chill at the heart of things or devouring flame about us. Frost is only a top dressing and fire a kindly light. Nature is uncommonly obliging. It may, of course, be argued that the explanation does not lie in nature, but in life; that we have evolved to suit our environment; that nature is not fitted to us, but that we have adapted to nature. In all, we have to agree that, our knowledge as a whole incomplete and likely to provide always a delight and challenge to the questing human spirit. We also have to agree that item by item of what we know seems to include a puckish reticence, and for each such item some compensating term or statistical average has to be invoked to accomplish our computing. Not only do our observations themselves affect our results, but, a hidden increment depletes them, and the precision of experiment must be followed by the rough usage of experience. That is why it is such a pity that applied science is so often separated from pure science in practice and status. The early and tragic troubles of the Comet aircraft show how technology, after all, is merely the ultimate laboratory.

Perhaps the greatest basic limitation of science emerges from the fact that, in its practices and its pronouncements, it must have standard units of measurements. To define is to constrain; and units infinitely divided lead to a corpuscular outlook. We see creation as particles; we cannot conceive of gradients, only as steps; nor of matter infinitely reducible to zero. Primary particles, quanta, photons, magnetrons, micro-seconds, gravitons-all nature is pulverized and we shift the little pieces. Indeed, few scientific hypotheses are exhaustive; almost all leave something out, and the reality behind the appearance eludes us however closely the latter has been examined by the most refined instruments. Not only is matter intractable, but it is contradictory. It has to be dealt with by mutually exclusive theories according to context, for example, as waves or as particles as appropriate.

Science can have little to say on the proposition that beauty is other than the items beautiful and truth an imprecision beyond the facts.

Certainly science can make abstractions from its realities-dimensions, shapes, durations, motion, mass; but it cannot make an abstraction of beauty or love etc. Only a poem can do that. Creative art is rightly so called because it makes what has not existed; it defies all quantitative limits. Truth may be finite. But beauty is without restriction; it belongs to the order of being that does not know quantity; for even if the number of originals could possibly be considered as limited, the number of reproductions (as in poems or novels) is inexhaustible; if the material for replicas were all used up, words, even repeated words, would remain to recall them and vision would rise to renew them. Beauty is infinitely producible.

Science and religion both seek within and beyond; they find no limits either way. Beyond seem to stretch infinity and eternity; strangely enough, the inwardness of things seems like those two incomprehensible extensions of space and time. The nuclear physicist, looking for the simple basis of matter, finds primary particles innumerable; so many particles as happenings; whorls of energy whose ultimate measures are rate and randomness. He has discovered antimatter and the other side of nothing; and he has seen matter that seems to run backwards in time. Looking as it were increasingly into the minute, it almost appears that he has reached zero and beyond into a negation of the spatial and the temporal that threatens to spread out into the obverse of infinity and eternity.

The scientist must, from these discoveries, question the basic scales with which he works. For instance, the existence of the infinitely negative must call in question the validity, in any final analysis, of an absolute scale of temperature that can only be positive; indeed, he already uses negative temperature, like multiple dimensions, for mathematical and logical sequences. Scientists are discovering, an infinite enclosed within a finite. And if there lies an infinite in the heart of the minute, what may lie within man who can already include the finite in his reasoning and embrace it in his logic? Religious men, of course, may go even further and suggest that what man can embrace, little more than man can encompass; they may even hint that man 'in the image of God' can be a simple statement after all, and that an anthropomorphic god may not, in the end, be inconceivable.

At any rate, both religious men and scientists can discern that, one way or another, in most things the dimensions are greater than the size. Perhaps the difference between science and religion can be better and more simply summed up by saying that science asks 'How?' while religion asks 'Why?'

Just as there are limitations of science, religion also has its limitations. Could it be that the ultimate reality is beyond the realms of these two domains?

6

Limitations of Religion

The first step towards the non-religion of the Western world was made by religion itself. When it defended its great symbols, not as symbols but as literal stories, it had already lost the battle.

- Paul Tillich (1886-1965). "The Lost Dimension in Religion", Saturday Evening Post, 14 June 1958.

It is my intention in this chapter to examine first the premises and logic which lead to it, and the purposes and ends which ensue, in order to discover whether between origins and results, religion contains any satisfaction for living people and any excuse for dead ones. I will begin with an examination of the origins and evolution of world religions and faith systems. How did religion begin? When a sufficient number of people so modify their wants as to make common prescription, then by force of numbers and numerical conditioning of environment they may reach exactly the mutual intention and approximately the individual wish. Such a body must, of course, give virtue to its objectives; it cannot induce participation or inspire its members without high purpose or, of course, high profits. People may work together to realize lesser aims when they conspire for a share of the loot. The common cause acquires a mythology, by which the enterprise is hallowed. And thus is religion, among such other things as state, regiment, trade union fostered.

Justification by faith has, therefore a more lowly origin than most theologians would wish to confess; but it need not be without a nobler reach. The religion that arises from the shared values of a culture can be burnished by time and experience. The household god may at first compete with the god of the Joneses next door; but the two finally embrace each other; and the new entity spreads in pious absorption into the faith of millions. The gods coalesce, the mythologies multiply. God has been made in the image of man, but man always wants more and better; he refines his deity; until in the end he has accomplished a bright instrument of revelation, and whatever god there be can wear that vision. And man reflected there is made in the image of god, whose voice from heaven may well say. 'This is my beloved son in whom I am well pleased'.

But there are other forces at work against this attainment. The community of faith, like any other community, is made up of people; and persons are both alone and unique. Each is the center of his own horizon; in time or place no other can be identified with any one. Someone may take my place when I move and, looking where I have looked, will find a world subtly altered by the passage of time; or he may stand near me and, looking where I am looking, will find a world slightly changed by the distance between us. His moment or slant must be different from mine. There is no absolute congruity in a world where time passes and views differ. For this reason there are potentially as many faiths as there are people, have been people and will be people.

We are born and we die one by one. We may come together, but we remain apart if only by the thickness of our skins. Because we are alone, we seek company; and we find companionship in common interests. As a result, where we are united in religion, we try to fix our devotions; we develop dogmas and postulate creeds, so that in these we are possessed of something mutual and unchanging. Alas that creed so often becomes the epitaph of dead faiths and liturgy its puppet-show. The light goes out as the tapers are lit and only shadows move and multiply. Religion becomes a thing of assumptions instead of the

94

enquiry that should follow from them. Truth is not assailed by prior belief.

Religion is mostly concerned with personal experiences and revelations. But personal experiences or perceptions are subjective. While our loneliness may thus stultify religion, our uniqueness undermines it. A consensus of opinion cannot take in the infinite variety of experience. The area of agreement is not and cannot be big enough to cover all that may happen to everyone. Therefore an area of agreement set out and held to its articles opposes its brittle compromise to the flexible weapons of single minds.

Religion as it stands is assumptive. There is not necessarily any harm in that, for one must begin somewhere. The trouble is that theology, the science or pseudo-science of religion, is more concerned to find where these assumptions lead than to unearth where they come from. It follows their consequences without questioning their validity and erects monumental belief upon untested foundations. Confirmation by experience may be fact, but not necessarily a truth. Man can live by faith whether true or false. And however fixed a man's belief, he can always fit events into it.

From the fact that religion is basically assumptive, instead of essentially explorative, come its limitations. A scientist may remit results which prove untenable, but a devotee of error must go back to its beginnings to start allover again. Assumptions, therefore, tend by their nature to be exclusive. They admit no contraries. This exclusiveness results in absurdities. A church- or those who represent it-argues from assumptions, although such assumptions have usually become so much absorbed into orthodoxy that they are not always recognized by those that hold them. In debate between churchman and unbeliever, the former generally comes off worse, because he argues from a brief the 'small print' of which he has not recently examined. His responses lack freedom. Like the politician or a trade unionist or any professional spokesman, his words are known before he utters them. He argues from a standpoint, not an issue. He is a boxer whose feet are shackled.

However lowly its origins-origins indeed symbolized in a manger; however immense its accretions of ancient superstitions; we cannot be sure that those origins and superstitions were not part of a fumbling towards reality: that, indeed, the likenesses between all religions old and new may not be their common ground of truth, and that their differences, however blown up by the hot air of fundamentalism, could not be pricked or floated off for the trivialities they are. Perhaps the religious way to enlightenment is the refining of belief rather than the discovery of fact. And in the deep strata of faith where buried gods still stir, we may yet sculpt a likeness of reality better than any idol yet carved by priestly knives.

Religious irrelevance is a factor of the survival of religion. It deals with an 'otherness' which cannot be destroyed by this world. And as men extend their world upwards and downwards and outwards and inwards, so heaven retreats to a new invulnerability. 'Pie in the sky' owes its value to the fact that it has not been tasted. Religion is beyond decay, disillusion and disproof; and so many of its followers try to keep it that way, by shrinking from the touch of knowledge, by science, for example, in evolution and by experience, for example, in spiritualism. Their faith, in the sense of unquestionable belief (and only at this low reckoning), is not so much the strength of its followers as the projection of their fears. Despite these weaknesses, religion does have some strength.

It is a strange fact that, out of the worst we do, remains the best that was in the deed. From the oppression that was Rome, comes the rule of law; upon the slave labor of Greece, was cultivated the flower of human thought; from the brutish ceremonies of barbarism came the ideal of self-sacrifice: Abraham the infanticide found a new and better light in the gleam of the pyre upon his lifted knife. It sometimes seems as if, from all human follies, only the good survives in the end. The aridities of philosophy and the fervors of superstition may be the bones and flesh respectively of the body of faith. One may suspect that somehow from that ill mating totters a semblance of truth.

Walter Taminang

A feeling of the sanctity of life is common to all men. Religious people impute it to an awareness of the godly spark within us and its Originator outside ourselves. Atheists consider it a natural response to the fact of our own vitality. I think it lies deeper than and before religion. But why should it persist in this age of physical interpretations? Has it been passed along the millennia by the overlap of generations or is it native to man? It is irrelevant to point to war and capital punishment as evidence contrary to the belief in the sanctity of human life. These things are not a negation, but an affirmation, a recognition that, because it is the ultimate in value, to threaten it is to exercise the ultimate in the coercion.

Forgive me for being blunt, but isn't it grossly arrogant for Christians or Muslims or adherents of other religious persuasions to believe that theirs is the only way to God? Why would any faith system think they are justified in asserting that they're right and that everybody else in the world is wrong? Anyone can claim to be the only path to God. The real issue is why anybody should believe them unquestioningly. Some people say that when you strip away all outer trappings, all the world religions are essentially teaching the universal fatherhood of God and the universal brotherhood of humankind. That would mean that all the world's faith systems are equally valid. Theologian John Hick said the world religions are different culturally conditioned responses to the ultimate 'Real,' or God. Isn't this like the old story of the three blind men feeling the elephant? Each religion is a sincere but inadequate attempt to explain the mystery of God, and so each one is valid in its own way. What is perceived by contemplation and revelation on earth is only an imperfect reflection of eternal truths and spiritual processes in the upper world of ultimate reality.

In a enthralling book, *Mysticism and Morality, A New Look At Old Questions* (Lanham: Lexington Books, 2004), Richard H. Jones [1] first shows that, far from religion being identical with or necessarily conducive to morality, the world religions have not only inspired violence, torture, wars, and injustice but by their very nature tend to construct value systems that "are legitimated by appeal to a religious authority and not by other-regardingness" A case in point is

Abraham's willingness to obey God's command and commit a patently immoral act by what Kierkegaard called a "'teleological suspension of the ethical in light of an overriding duty to obey God's will" Jones continues, "Basing one's actions on personal consequences is by definition not other-regarding, and thus a person acting only out of religious obligation is not being moral, regardless of the positive consequences to others, but non-moral or even immoral" However, Jones is quick to point out that people can simultaneously "act both out of a religious concern for themselves and a moral concern for others" and concludes, "A religious value-system must be deemed non-moral unless it can be shown to be otherwise" However, Jones goes on:

> Religious worldviews, as part of their function of legitimizing the value-system of a culture, can provide a framework in which morality makes sense and is the highest social vision. This makes the context of religious other-impinging action-guides different from that of nonreligious ones: the action-guides become part of the religious demands on a person. In sum, a religion can provide reasons and motives for being moral, even if morality is logically autonomous.

Through the centuries, the world has seen plenty of acrimony and violence over differences in the way people view God. Disgusted by religious bickering, some people have thrown up their hands and said the world would be a much better place if people simply stopped arguing over doctrinal disputes and instead focused on living in peace with each other. There are moral-living Muslims, Jews, Christians, Mormons, Buddhists, and Hindus. Isn't how a person lives and treats his neighbor more important than what he believes theologically? People say Gandhi lived a more virtuous life than most of today's believers. Why would he be sent to hell just because he wasn't a follower of Jesus or Mohammed for instance? Isn't it unfair to condemn hundreds of millions of Muslims and believers of other creeds, when they never heard about Jesus and merely followed the religious traditions of their parents? One of the basic tenets of most religions and belief systems is that we humans can survive our own death and even maintain our physical forms in an after-life, in which we will meet and recognize our resurrected ancestors. The next chapter examines the basis of these beliefs.

7

The Realm Beyond

Follow me; and let the dead bury their dead.

- Mathew 8:22 (KJV)

The afterlife or life after death is a broad term for a continuation of existence after death, typically in a spiritual or ghostlike afterworld. The major views on the afterlife derive from religion, esotericism and metaphysics. Scientists of the materialist-reductionist extraction are skeptical of the existence of the afterlife, stating that the topic is supernatural, and therefore does not really exist or is unknowable.

In metaphysical models, theists generally believe some sort of afterlife awaits people when they die. Atheists generally believe that there is not a life after death. Members of some generally non-theistic religions such as Buddhism, tend to believe in an afterlife like reincarnation but without reference to God. Agnostics generally hold the position that like the existence of God, the existence of supernatural phenomena, such as souls or life after death, is unverifiable and therefore unknowable. Some philosophies (i.e. post humanism, Humanism, and often empiricism) generally hold that there is not an afterlife. Many religions, whether they believe in the soul's existence in another world like Christianity, Islam and many pagan belief systems, or in reincarnation like many forms of Hinduism and Buddhism, believe that one's status in the afterlife is a reward or punishment for their conduct during life. To the extent that the afterlife is a form of justice, it is usually restricted to humans, as animals are not held responsible for their actions.

Modern science, in general, either describes the universe and human beings without reference to a soul or to an afterlife, or tends to remain mute on the issue. A notable exception is a famous study conducted in 1901 by physician Duncan MacDougall, who sought to measure the weight purportedly lost by a human body when the soul departed the body upon death. [1] MacDougall weighed dying patients in an attempt to prove that the soul was material, tangible and thus measurable. These experiments are widely considered to have had little if any scientific merit, and although MacDougall's results varied considerably from "21 grams," for some people this figure has become synonymous with the measure of a soul's mass. The title of the 2003 movie *21 Grams* is a reference to MacDougall's findings.

Others, such as Francis Crick in 1994, have attempted a 'scientific search for the soul'[2.] Frank Tipler has argued that physics can explain immortality, though such arguments are not falsifiable and thus do not qualify as science. Some investigations have been conducted which failed to find evidence that "out-of-body" experiences transcend the confines of the brain. For example, one hospital placed an LED marquee above its patients' beds which displayed a hidden message that could only be read if one were looking down from above. As of 2001, no one who claimed near-death experience or out-of-body experience within that hospital had reported having seen the hidden message. [3]

Near Death Experiences

Improved medical technology and treatment have brought more people back from death's door than ever before. As a result, more survivors are reporting near-death experiences (NDEs). Usually they are patients who survive cardiac arrest, coma, near fatal trauma, near drowning, or some other severe illness. Yet there are also cases of NDEs resulting from catastrophic psychological stress not involving physical injury. Examples of this are survivors of mountain climbing accidents and miners trapped for days after cave-ins.

There's a great deal of confusion about the so-called 'near–death experience" Medical and behavioral scientific research is divided as to whether whatever is experienced is a hallucination, a product of mass hysteria, a chemical reaction in the brain due to traumatic stress, or truly a stage between life and death. Probably the first case of a near-death experience was reported by the ancient Greek philosopher Plato (427-347 B.C). In The republic, Plato tells of a soldier named Er who was supposedly killed in battle. As the account goes, while Er lay on the battlefield, his soul took flight. Accompanied by the souls of several fellow soldiers, Er's soul experienced another world - a land where all souls were judged. He saw other souls choosing their subsequent incarnations and then drinking from the River of Forgetfulness in order to obliterate their past memories. But Er was forbidden to drink, and then he blacked out. He revived into his real, conscious life just in time as his funeral pyre was lit.

Popular interest in near-death experiences was initially sparked by Raymond Moody, Jr's 1975 book, *Life after Life* and the founding of the International Association for Near-Death Studies (IANDS) in 1978 taking his cue from another work *Return from Tomorrow* by George G. Ritchie, M.D. with Elizabeth Sherrill (1978). At the age of twenty, George Ritchie died in an army hospital. Nine minutes later he returned to life. What happened to him during those minutes was so compelling, it changed his life forever. In *Return from Tomorrow*, he tells of his out-of-the-body encounter with other beings, his travel through different dimensions of time and space, and ultimately, his transforming meeting with the Light of the world, the Son of God, Jesus Christ. Ritchie's extraordinary experience not only altered his view of eternity, it directed and governed his entire life, and provided a startling and hopeful description of the realm beyond. Ritchie's story was the first contact Dr. Raymond Moody, PhD (who was studying at the University of Virginia, as an undergraduate in Philosophy, at the time) had with NDEs. It inspired Moody to investigate over 150 cases of near-death experiences, in his book *Life After Life*, and two other books that followed.

The phenomenology of an NDE usually includes physiological, psychological and alleged transcendental aspects. Typically, the experience follows a distinct progression:

1. A sense of being dead; the sudden awareness that one has had a "fatal" accident or failed to survive an operation.
2. Peace and painlessness; A feeling that the ties that bind one to the world have been cut.
3. An out-of-body experience; the sensation of peering down on one's own body and perhaps seeing doctors and nurses attempting resuscitation.
4. Tunnel experience; the sense of moving up or through a narrow passageway.
5. "People of light"; being met at the end of the tunnel by others who are "glowing"
6. "Being of light"; the presence of a God-like figure or force of some kind.
7. Panoramic life view; being shown one's life by the "Being of light".
8. Reluctance to return; the feeling of being comfortable and surrounded by the "light", often described as "pure love".
9. Personality transformation; a psychological change involving loss of fear of death, greater spiritualism, a sense of "connectedness" with the earth, and a greater zest for life.

Of these, the most frequent element in the near-death experience is by far the out-of-body experience. Perhaps 75 percent of reported NDEs involve an out-of-body experience. The second most frequent element is the so-called "panoramic life review". As the term suggests, the events in one's entire life flash by in the mind in an instant. In order of diminishing frequency, the other common features of NDEs include entering a tunnel, meeting others (such as living or dead relatives), encountering a " Being of light", having a sense of the presence of " a deity," returning to the body, and experiencing what researchers call " elements of depersonalization" (such as an altered sense of time or detachment from reality). Some people have also experienced extremely distressing NDEs, which can manifest in forewarning of emptiness or a sense of dread towards the cessation of their life in its current state.

According to the Rasch Scale, a "core" near-death experience encompasses peace, joy, and harmony, followed by insight and mystical or religious experiences. The most intense NDEs are reported to have an awareness of things occurring in a different place or time, and some of these observations are said to have been evidential. Another interesting finding is that there is an extraordinary similarity in the backgrounds of those who report having a near-death experience: there is a "consistent tendency" for these people to have also reported being victims of child abuse.

Many theories explaining near-death experiences abound, and many studies are teasing out the myths from the reality. Another interesting finding in recent years is that there is a large cultural component in NDEs. Which elements are more likely to appear differs according to the society in which a person was brought up. For example, based on the work of Dr. NSama Mumwe of the department of Psychology at the University of Zambia, it has been noted that Africans reporting an NDE see the experience as evil and involving witchcraft. Among Japanese who have an NDE, many report seeing long, dark rivers and beautiful flowers, which are common symbols in Japanese art. And East Indians sometimes see a "bureaucracy" in their vision of heaven. Finally, Micronesians sometimes see heaven as a large city with skyscrapers.

Dr Kenneth Ring [4,5] has identified twelve changes that often occur in a person *after* a near-death experience:

1. A greater appreciation of life
2. A higher self-esteem
3. A great compassion for others
4. A heightened sense of purpose and self-understanding
5. A desire to learn
6. An elevated spirituality
7. A greater ecological sensitivity
8. A feeling of being more intuitive, sometimes "psychic"
9. An increased physical sensitivity
10. A diminished tolerance to light, alcohol, and drugs

11. A feeling that his or her brain has been "altered" to encompass more
12. A feeling that he or she is now using the "whole brain" rather than just a small part.

Biological Analysis and Theories

In the 1990s, Dr. Rick Strassman conducted research on the psychedelic drug Dimethyltryptamine (DMT) at the University of New Mexico. Strassman advanced the theory that a massive release of DMT from the pineal gland prior to death or near-death was the cause of the near-death experience phenomenon. Only two of his test subjects reported NDE-like aural or visual hallucinations, although many reported feeling as though they had entered a state similar to the classical NDE. His explanation for this was the possible lack of panic involved in the clinical setting and possible dosage differences between those administered and those encountered in actual NDE cases. All subjects in the study were also very experienced users of DMT and/or other psychedelic/entheogenic agents. Some speculators consider that if subjects without prior knowledge on the effects of DMT been used during the experiment, that it is possible more volunteers would have reported feeling as though they had experienced an NDE.

Critics have argued that neurobiological models often fail to explain NDEs that result from close brushes with death, where the brain does not actually suffer physical trauma, such as a near-miss automobile accident. Such events may however have neurobiological effects caused by stress.
In a new theory devised by Kinseher in 2006, the knowledge of the Sensory Autonomic System is applied in the NDE phenomenon. His theory states that the experience of looming death is an extremely strange paradox to a living organism - and therefore it will start the NDE: during the NDE, the individual becomes capable of "seeing" the brain performing a scan of the whole episodic memory (even prenatal experiences), in order to find a stored experience which is comparable to the input information of death. All these scanned and retrieved bits of information are permanently evaluated by the actual mind, as it is

searching for a coping mechanism out of the potentially fatal situation. Kinseher feels this is the reason why a near-death experience is so unusual.

The theory also states that out-of-body experiences, accompanied with NDEs, are an attempt by the brain to create a mental overview of the situation and the surrounding world. The brain then transforms the input from sense organs and stored experience (knowledge) into a dream-like idea about oneself and the surrounding area. Whether or not these experiences are hallucinatory, they do have a profound impact on the observer. Many psychologists not necessarily pursuing the paranormal, such as Susan Blackmore, have recognized this. These scientists are not trying to debunk the experience, so much so as searching for biological reasons that cause an NDE. Near-death experiences can have tremendous effects on the people who have them, their families, and medical workers.

Spiritual Viewpoints

Some view the NDE the precursor to an afterlife experience, claiming that the NDE cannot be completely explained by physiological or psychological causes, and that consciousness can function independently of brain activity. [7] Many NDE-accounts seem to include elements which, according to several theorists, can only be explained by an out-of-body consciousness. For example, in one account, a woman accurately described a surgical instrument she had not seen previously, as well as a conversation that occurred while she was under general anesthesia. [8] In another account, from a proactive Dutch NDE study, a nurse removed the dentures of an unconscious heart attack victim, and was asked by him after his recovery to return them. It might be difficult to explain in conventional terms how an unconscious patient could later have recognized the nurse. [9]
Dr. Michael Sabom reports a case about a woman who underwent surgery for an aneurysm. The woman reported an out-of-body experience that she claimed continued through a brief period of the absence of any EEG activity. If true, this would seem to challenge the belief by many that consciousness is situated entirely within the brain. [10]

A majority of individuals who experience an NDE see it as a verification of the existence of an afterlife. This includes those with agnostic/atheist inclinations before the experience. Many former atheists, such as the Reverend Howard Storm [11] have adopted a more spiritual viewpoint after their NDEs. Howard Storm's NDE might also be characterized as a distressing near-death experience. The distressing aspects of some NDE's are discussed more closely by Greyson & Bush (1992). Greyson claims that "No one physiological or psychological model by itself explains all the common features of NDE. The paradoxical occurrence of heightened, lucid awareness and logical thought processes during a period of impaired cerebral perfusion raises particular perplexing questions for our current understanding of consciousness and its relation to brain function. A clear sensorium and complex perceptual processes during a period of apparent clinical death challenge the concept that consciousness is localized exclusively in the brain." [12] A few people feel that research on NDEs occurring in the blind can be interpreted to support an argument that consciousness survives bodily death.

Having come this far, I hope the reader would now be ready to tackle the "big questions" that prompted the writing of this book: Why am I alive? What is the point of my existence? What is my purpose on earth? What do I do with my life? Is my existence just an accident? Such questions have haunted mankind since the beginning of time and form the basis of most philosophical and religious inquiry.

8

The Meaning of Life

Be not afraid of life. Believe that life is worth living, and your belief will help create the fact.
                                                            -William James

It is very reasonable for humans to want to understand something of our context in a broader universe, awesome and vast. It is also reasonable for us to want to understand something about ourselves. Leo Tolstoy, writing in *Anna Karenina* says "without knowing what I am and why I am here, life is impossible." If we find life literally impossible without answering that question, at least life's difficulties increase.

How important to you is the on-going survival of humankind? How important to you is the on-going survival of your country? How important to you is the on-going survival of your friends and family? And how important is it to you that you remain alive - and live long? Enthusiasm for living is the driving force behind the desire to live. I personally find live intriguing and challenging. The present world is such a rich treasure-store of marvelous opportunities. Given that the vast majority of people who could potentially be thrown up by the combinatorial lottery of DNA will in fact never be born, we are staggeringly lucky to find ourselves in the spotlight. However brief and transient our time here on earth, if we waste a second of it, or complain that it is dull or barren or boring, couldn't it be seen as a callous insult to those unborn trillions who will never even be offered life in the first place?

But then one might ask "How can a life that ends have meaning?" One individual's life can have value, simply because of the enjoyment of that individual. It is the experience of life itself which has meaning. One might say that it is the limited nature of life which makes it so valuable. Everyone has heard of people who were told by their doctor that they only had a short time to live. They are usually advised to "make the most" of the time they have left. This is because the value of each day has just increased due to its new status as a rare commodity (supply and demand). Have you ever considered what the abysmal value of an infinite life would be? It seems to me that many immortal people would eventually commit suicide. What would not be boring to you after 1,000 years, or a million?

Being alive in this universe is an incredible opportunity to experience and explore as many things as one possibly can. By setting goals and attaining them, by participating in meaningful projects, by providing for loved ones, by overcoming adversity, one can certainly find great fulfillment in life. But telling people what I would do with my life may not satisfy those who don't know what to do with theirs. Some people by virtue of their life circumstances or their genetic predisposition just don't seem to have much enthusiasm for life. They complain often, curse, blame others or themselves at the slightest inconvenience, are sluggish and often are sad and depressed.

You may never be able to make yourself happy or sad or indifferent by an act of will, but you can always choose to locate your emotions on a bigger map: the map of the nobility of your existence, even in the face of its impermanence. Every person can experience the wonder of being alive, and episodes of sadness reinforce our appreciation of the happy moments. Think of yourself as a majestic mountain in the vast human range.

In my opinion, the overall purpose of life is the development of spiritual competence. In chapter two we looked at the concept of evolution; just as physical evolution is concerned with increasing physical competence, spiritual growth is concerned with the evolution of the human spirit. Throughout our lives, our spiritual competence can improve until the moment of death. The process of evolution as we know it is a miracle because it violates one of the fundamental laws of nature, the second law of thermodynamics or the law of entropy. This law states that energy naturally flows from a state of greater organization to a state of lesser organization or from a state of higher differentiation to a state of lower differentiation. Since the process of evolution leads to increased levels of organization, it runs counter to natural law. In the ordinary course of things, nothing in the physical universe should exist due to entropy. Therefore we owe our very existence on earth to this unnatural; I dare say *mysterious* negation of natural law.

So what is this thrusting force that has consistently driven the evolutionary process for billions and billions of years? Of what necessity is evolution? I think that the driving force behind our physical and spiritual evolution is a higher power which I will call God. To what end is this God-directed process? This troubling question has undoubtedly caused sleepless nights to many a white-bearded sage over the millennia. I have also spent considerable time pondering on its possible answer and implications. Now, let's look at it this way: Due to the fact that we humans are the highest evolved beings known, could it be God put us here on earth in order that we should gradually perfect ourselves and become more and more like Him. Looked at from this perspective our life on earth then becomes a God-given opportunity to develop physically and spiritually, permitting us to align ourselves more and more with God's overall plan? What then is spiritual growth?

Spiritual growth can be described as the never-ending process of evolution of our consciousness, or the continuous refinement of each individual's self-awareness. The more evolved our consciousness, the more we understand the purpose of our existence and how we fit into the overall cosmic reality. A more refined self-awareness and sense of purpose leads to a better understanding of our relationship to other people, our surroundings, and the consequences of our actions and non-actions. In other words, as we grow spiritually, we become more capable of distinguishing between good and evil. We find it easier to overcome our lethargy and natural apathy, leading to a gradual expansion in our capacity to love and be loved. In other words, our evolved consciousness empowers us to give full expression to the love of God that is present within each and everyone of us.

The purpose of life thus becomes the attainment of godhead by the conscious self. When we can identify our mature free will with that of God, when we become capable of making independent choices that influence the world, we will have assumed through our conscious mind, a new and vibrant life form. We will have become partners with God, so to speak. God wants us to use our time on this earth to evolve spiritually, evolve god consciousness, and partner with Him in the never-ending creation process.

EPILOGUE

Until a century ago, it was possible for people to spend all or most of their lives without having to deal with "others" who live by very different belief systems and principles. This is no longer an option, and humanity must learn to overcome the long ingrained habit of viewing others primarily as subjects to be "converted" to *our* ways. For millennia we had been taught that the "other," the "outsider," the one who is "different," is by definition dangerous and in need of correction until he or she is more like "us." If humanity is to survive and flourish in an environment that renders cultural and geographic isolation impossible, it is essential that the world religions become active forces for compassion, love, and justice. Only by learning to put things in proper perspective can we hope to stem the tide of global religious fundamentalism that is threatening to annihilate us all.

In this book, we have examined the different tools - religion, science, and philosophy - that mankind has used to answer the difficult questions of our existence, and shown how these tools overlap and complement each other, their limitations and the potential to cause conflicts. We further examined how science and religion help in our understanding of the origins of life and the mystery of creation. We determined that, while science can help us to understand the convoluted process that led to the emergence of complex, sentient humans, religion strengthens the faith necessary for us to grapple with questions like "what preceded the big bang?" and "what is the meaning of life?" Apart from explaining our origins and complexity, a good understanding of evolution also enables us to come to grips with the common ancestry of all humans. The recognition that all humans are kin can improve the way we perceive and treat each other, thus lessening inter-religious and other types of bickering, with enormous potential benefits to our species. We then explored the major world religions and their common beliefs and practices, to enable us determine their common ground and possibilities for non-violent co-existence. Bearing in mind that the belief in life-after-death forms the fulcrum of most religions and belief systems we examined the phenomenon of near-death experiences, their importance in our quest for spiritual enlightenment, and how these experiences provide a glimpse into the hereafter. This book attempts to provide a framework on how we can transcend our belief systems and live harmoniously in the 21st century and beyond.

NOTES

Prologue

1. http://aps.naples.net/community/NFNWebpages/
storyboard.cfm?StoryBoardNum=142&PageNum=1
Center for reduction of religious-based conflicts: Accessed
   01/08/2008.
2. World Christian database.
3. The Economist November 3rd-9th 2007."*The new wars of religion*"
   p 95.

Chapter 1: The Search for Truth

1. Quotation: "The conflict thesis, at least in its simple form, is now
   widely perceived as a wholly inadequate intellectual framework
   within which to construct a sensible and realistic historiography of
   Western science." (p. 7), from the essay by Colin A. Russell "*The
   Conflict Thesis*" on "Gary Ferngren (editor). Science & Religion:
   A Historical Introduction. Baltimore: Johns Hopkins University
   Press, 2002. ISBN 0-8018-7038-0".

Chapter 2: The Origins of Life

1. Chris Gunter, Ritu Dhand. "*The Mouse Genome*" Nature 420
   (05 Dec. 2004) p.509

Chapter 3: Evolution and Religion

1. "*Moses wrote the Book of Genesis*", also at:
   http://www.reformation.org/
2. A.D. White, "The *History of the Warfare of Science with
   Theology in Christendom,*" Prometheus Books, Buffalo NY,
   (1993; reprint of the 1896 original), P. 27.
3. Kitty Ferguson, "*The Fire in the Equations: Science, religion
   and the Search for God,*" Eardmans, Grand Rapids, MI, (1995),
   Page 261.

4. Pope John Paul II, *"Truth cannot contradict truth,"* 1996-OCT-22, at: http://www.csn.net/
5. Pope Pius XII, "*Humani Generis,*" at: http://www.shrine.com/
6. David Cloud, "*Pope Supports Evolution,*" at http://www.whidbey.net/
7. News release, Vatican Information Service, 1996-OCT-23, at: http://www.reformation.org

Chapter 4: Major World Religions

1. Fowler, Jeaneane D. *World Religions:An Introduction for Students.* Pp 56-57,59. Sussex Academic Press (1997). ISBN 1898723486.
2. http://http://www.bbc.co.uk/religion/religions/christianity/ Accessed 01/20/2008
3. Britannica Encyclopedia, *Jihad*
4. *The Concise Oxford Dictionary of World Religions.* Ed. John Bowker. Oxford University Press, 2000; The term can be traced to late 19th century Hindu reform movements (J. Zavos, Defending Hindu Tradition: Sanatana Dharma as a Symbol of Orthodoxy in Colonial India, Religion (Academic Press), Volume 31, Number 2, April 2001, pp. 109-123; see also R. D. Baird, *Swami Bhaktivedanta and the Encounter with Religions, Modern Indian Responses to Religious Pluralism*, edited by Harold Coward, State University of New York Press, 1987).
5. *Polytheism.* Encyclopædia Britannica. Encyclopædia Britannica Online (2007). Retrieved on 01/19/2008
6. Smith 1991, p. 64
7. Bhagavad Gita 2.22
8. Rinehart 2004, pp. 19–21
9. There are within theology two opposing traditions in this regard: one, the *doctrine of Emanence*, which holds that grace emanates down from an external God to men; the other, the *doctrine of Immanence*, which holds that grace immanates out from the God within the core of man's being.
10. Bhaskarananda 1994, p. 112

11. Krishnakumar, R.. "*Beef without borders*", Frontline, Narasimhan Ram, August 30-September 12, 2003. Retrieved on 01/23/2007

12. Sri Swami Sivananda, "*Lord Buddha,*" (1996), at: http://www.sivanandadlshq.org/

13. Charles Prebish & Damien Keown, "*Buddhism* - the eBook. Chapter 2," at: http://www.jbeonlinebooks.org/

14. This is the popular, short version of the Thirteen Principles. The original, more complete, version appears in the book: Rambam's Commentary on the Mishnah.

15. Salk J: *The Survival of the Wisest.* New York, Harper & Row, 1973.

16. Vladimir Tomek "*General observations on religion by a religious liberal*" (2006) at http://www.religioustolerance.org/tomek23.htm: Accessed 25th January 2008

Chapter 5: Limitations of Religion

1. Richard H. Jones '*Mysticism and Morality, A New Look At Old Questions*' (Lanham: Lexington Books, 2004).

Chapter 6: The Realm Beyond

1. Roach, Mary (2005). Spook – *Science Tackles the Afterlife.* W. W. Norton & Co. ISBN 0-393-05962-6.

2. Crick, Francis (1995). *The Astonishing Hypothesis – the Scientific Search for the Soul.* Touchstone Books. ISBN 0-684-80158-2

3. Alper, Matthew (2001). *The "God" Part of the Brain - a Scientific Interpretation of Human Spirituality and God.* Rogue Press. ISBN 0-9660367-0-0.

4. Ring, Kenneth: "*Heading toward Omega. In search of the Meaning of Near-Death Experience*", 1984.

5. Ring, K. "*Life at death. A scientific investigation of the near-death experience.*" 1980, New York: Coward McCann and Geoghenan.

6. Bruce Greyson, Kevin Nelson, Susan Blackmore, webpage: News-wdeath11-2006-04.
7. Rivas, 2003
8. Sabom, Michael. *Light & Death: One Doctor's Fascinating Account of Near-Death Experiences*. 1998. Grand Rapids, Michigan: Zondervan Publishing House
9. Van Lommel P, van Wees R, Meyers V, Elfferich I. (2001) *Near-Death Experience in Survivors of Cardiac Arrest: A prospective Study in the Netherlands*. Lancet, December 15; 358(9298):2039-45.
10. Sabom, Michael. *Light & Death: One Doctor's Fascinating Account of Near-Death Experiences*. 1998. Grand Rapids, Michigan: Zondervan Publishing House.
11. Rodrigues, 2004
12. Greyson, 2001

Books and Journals

- W. H.. Boore, *First Light,* Search Press, London, 1973, ISBN 0855323159.
- Schubert M. Ogden, *The Reality of God And Other Essays,* Harper & Row, Publishers, New York1977, ISBN 0-06-066351-0
- Lou Marinoff, *The Big Questions: How Philosophy can Change your Life,* Bloomsbury, 2003, ISBN 1-58234-253-9.
- Rick Warren, *The Purpose Driven Life: What on Earth Am I Here For?* Zondervan, 2002, ISBN: 0-310-20571-9.
- Alberto Villoldo, *The Four Insights: Wisdom, Power and Grace of the Earthkeepers,* Hay House, Inc, 2006, ISBN: 978-1-4019-1045-7.
- Carl sagan, *The Varieties of Scientific Experience: A personal view of the Search for God,* The Penguin Press, 2006, ISBN: 1-59420-107-2.
- Richard Dawkins, *The God Delusion,* Bantam Press, 2006, ISBN-13:978-0-618-68000-9.
- Francis S. Collins, *The Language of God*: Free Press, 2006, ISBN 978-0-7432-8639-8.
- John Brockman, *Intelligent Thought: Science versus the intelligent Design* Movement vintage Books, 2006, ISBN-10: 0-307-27722-4.
- Stephen R. Covey *The 7 Habits of Highly Effective People: Powerful Lessons in Personal Change*, Fireside, New York, 19890-671-70863-5.
- Mary Roach, *Spook, Science Tackles the Afterlife*, W.W. Norton & Company, Inc, 2005, ISBN 0-393-05962-6.
- M. Scott Peck, *The Road Less Travelled: The New Psychology of Love, Traditional Values and Spiritual Growth,* Hutchinson &Co. Great Britain, 1985, ISBN 0 09 972740 4.

Walter Taminang

www.ingramcontent.com/pod-product-compliance
Lightning Source LLC
LaVergne TN
LVHW091155080426
835509LV00006B/700